The Audacious Adventures of
Zazoo Plazz

The Audacious Adventures of
Zazoo Plazz

*Part-time Superhero,
Full-time Mom*

By Leslie B. Placzek

Copyright © 2020 Leslie Bilodeau Placzek

Publisher's Cataloging-in-Publication Data
Names: Placzek, Leslie Bilodeau, author.
Title: The Audacious adventures of Zazoo Plazz, part-time superhero, full-time mom / by Leslie Bilodeau Placzek.
Description: Includes bibliographical references | Leslie Bilodeau Placzek: South Windsor, CT, 2020.
Identifiers: LCCN: 2020900247 | ISBN: 978-1-7344297-0-1
Subjects: LCSH Placzek, Leslie Bilodeau. | Motherhood--United States--Anecdotes, facetiae, satire, etc.| Mother and child--United States--Anecdotes, facetiae, satire, etc. | Working mothers--United States--Biography. | Conduct of life--Humor. | Hartford (Conn.)--Biography. | BISAC HUMOR / Form / Essays | BIOGRAPHY & AUTOBIOGRAPHY / Personal Memoirs
Classification: LCC HQ759 .P562 2020 | DDC 306.8/743--dc23

All Rights Reserved. No part of this publication may be reproduced, stored in a retrieval system, or transmitted in any form or by any means, electrical, mechanical, photocopying, recording or otherwise, without the prior written consent of the author.

Cover design: Robin Tatlow-Lord
Editor: Kathryn Cartwright
Layout: Karen Tants

All photographs are from the author's collection. Some names and identifying details of people and places described in this book have been altered to protect their privacy. Though all events recounted in this book actually occurred, the author assumes all responsibility for exaggerations and aggrandizements.

Copyright of the articles/essays listed within this book belong to the author, as a student writer. You will find these listed in the endnotes.
1. "The Real Steele," by Leslie Bilodeau, published in the December 19, 1980 edition of the *ECHO*, student newspaper of East Catholic High School, 115 New State Road, Manchester, Connecticut 06042
2. "The Real Steele," by Leslie Bilodeau, published in the 1981 *ECLAT*, the student literary arts magazine of East Catholic High School, 115 New State Road, Manchester, Connecticut 06042

3. Note: The author refers to this book in a story (but doesn't quote from it): *Bob Steele, A Man and His Humor*, Copyright 1980 by Spoonwood Press, P. O. Box 3153 Hartford, Connecticut 06103.

DEDICATION

This book is dedicated to my fellow
Part-time Superheroes and Full-time Moms.

To all of you bright lights
Stuck in the middle
Tending the fires, minding the griddle
Waiting in minivans, eyes on your phone
Socially networked, yet oh, so alone
Saving the world one day at a time
The paycheck too small to save but a dime
Midafternoon you stifle a yawn,
Sleepless at midnight, but up with the dawn
This is the time, though it all seems so wild
To go back, reclaim the lost, lovely child
Who's waiting to whisper into your ear
The thing you've forgotten but once held so dear.

ACKNOWLEDGEMENTS

Stretched across my computer's home screen is a scene from Matthew's gospel (Chapter 14, verses 22-33), in the New Testament of the Bible. A thunderstorm rages on the sea, rocking the apostles' fishing boat, as Peter sinks to his knees in the water. He seems oblivious to Jesus—perched on a wave two feet away—who extends his hand calmly in Peter's direction. Gazing at the scene, I thank Jesus, the Holy Spirit, and my angels and wise spirit guides for supporting and inspiring me on my journey to fulfill God's plan for my life, especially when I begin to question why I left the comfort of my nice, dry boat.

God's support comes in many forms, including the people who've popped up in my life to steer me in the right direction at the right time, or to teach me a lesson. Some of those people appear in this book (in disguise), and a few guided me from behind the scenes. Other folks may turn up in my next book, the third, or fourth. Thanks to my husband (GP)--my three-legged race partner--for your support, precise and heartfelt feedback, and patience, which made it possible for me to fulfill my dream of bringing Zazoo Plazz to life on the page—and in person.

To my sons (BP and ZP), I offer this bit of advice I got from a fortune cookie (which I taped to my primitive design of a pot of gold at the end of a rainbow): "Be Brave Enough to Live Creatively." In other words, fight to keep your "sacred space," even when people make fun of your white sage "aura smudge" purifying room spray.

I give a high five paw to Bebe, my Devoted Dog, for staying close by my side at those times when you have nothing to gain but a rub behind the ears or a kiss on the nose, and for having the decency to leave me the last slice of pizza.

I am eternally grateful to Julie Ann Turner[1] (my creative guide and Mama Bear at the top of the cliff), without whom this book--and Zazoo herself-- would still be a jumble of memories in my heart, and the legions of butterflies in my head would be crashing into my ears instead of spiraling upward infinitely in perfect unison. Finding you was *my* epiphany.

To Robin Tatlow-Lord, my creative colleague from Down Under, for her brilliant cover illustration, her willingness to adapt her own "Bobby Dazzler" roller derby superhero and dog into Zazoo Plazz and "DD," and for adding the "extras." I am so glad the stars aligned for us to work together, and I'm excited to collaborate with you again soon on the next Zazoo project!

This book went from "rough" to "ready" thanks to the patience, expertise, and loving critique of my editor, Kathryn Cartwright, and the formatting flair of her Australian colleague, author Karen Tants at Healing Pen Publishing.

Special thanks to Arti Roots Ross at Chrysalis Springs in Richmond, Massachusetts, for hosting a glorious autumn weekend retreat. Meeting you and our fellow "pilgrims" sparked an idea for the second *Zazoo* book and led me to consider starting an annual tradition of pre-birthday adventure weekends!

Heartfelt thanks to my fellow visionaries throughout the world, connected through technology. Though we've never met, I feel like you are family. You lift me up when the crabs are trying to pull me back down into the bucket.

I am grateful to my parents and extended family, for establishing the perfect environment for little Zazoo, the budding writer, to flourish, and also for providing me with so much wonderful material.

Thanks to my mother-in-law (IP), with permission--finally--to show this book to everyone in your town.

To my friends, neighbors, co-workers, and acquaintances, for being my sounding board, even when I had no wine to offer in return. Special gratitude goes out to my dental hygienist, who typically spends an hour and a half cleaning my teeth while allowing for my random rants and asides--like my unhealthy obsession with those little green dental picks that regularly spill out of their zipper pouch and into the abyss of my handbag, never to be seen again.

With love to "All the Souls" of those who have guided me on my path and continue to inspire me today, especially: Memere and Pepere Belanger; Granny and Grandpa Bilodeau; Uncle Maurice "Moe" Belanger; and Mr. H. Allen Greer, my high school English teacher and mentor.

Contents

Dedication 7

Acknowledgements 9

Prologue 15
A Day in the Life of Zazoo Plazz, Part-time Superhero, Full-time Mom

Preface 21
Hey, What's So Funny? 25
Nobody Puts Leslie in a Crib 29
Bright Light 33
Part-Time Private Eye 37
Pardon My French 43
Going With the Flow 49
Don't Eat the Toothpicks! 55
Part-time Passion for Fashion 59
Kitchen Explorations 67
As I Sew, So Shall I Weep 71
It Just Makes Scents 75
Zazoo's Pen Plazz 81
Next Life Savings and Loan 85
Perplexed Planetary Pupil 91
Hair Apparent 97
Great (Mrs.) Scott! 103
Nerves of 'Steele' 107
Schools of Swimming (S.O.S.) 113

I Love It in the Yoga Zone:

Wherever I Lay My Mat is My Om...........................117

The Stride Hyper of Smellingdung..........................123

(Not So) Hot to Trot..127

Miss Merry Moonwalk 137

Focus on Your Calling 145

Cleaning Troubles, Oils and Grumbles 151

The Lollipop Ladies 157

Three in the Afternoon 163

Full of Beans...167

The Juggler...171

Inside Information...177

Bumpers and the Blarney Stone...............................181

Fair Opal Starstamp 189

Welcome to Room 125..197

Settle Down, Sally..205

Uncle Mabel Anger..215

Leo Joseph and the Eight-Sided Table.....................221

Zazoo Plazz, Zealous Performer 231

The Banjo Nose Best..239

The Aquarian Centenarian 245

Epilogue..**251**

Doggie Drama--and Dharma

Endnotes **255**

PROLOGUE

A Day in the Life of Zazoo Plazz,
Part-time Superhero, Full-time Mom

In January 2018, I made a commitment to myself to assemble my stories into this book and release it into the world within a year. Everything was on schedule, planets aligned, the universe providing, creative ideas like butterflies fluttering into formation, and then, in mid-April, I hit a couple of bumps in the road. The following account is an accurate depiction of how my "expressing my gifts in the world" train easily derailed over my sons' spring school vacation week.

That Wednesday, I had envisioned getting up at four thirty to meditate, exercise, shower, and have a nice, relaxing breakfast, settling in at my desk to write by seven with a hot cup of tea. Ha!

Here's what really happened:

With my husband, Gray, up half the night preparing for a business trip, and son, Brenin, up until four playing computer games, I slept fitfully, waking with a start at six thirty (Mercury retrograde messed with my alarm, or I sleepwalked and slammed it against the wall). Sprang out of bed like a rocket and threw on workout clothes. Once down in basement workout corner, overpowered by chocolate smell emanating from empty bag of crunchy chocolate Easter eggs in 'man cave' trash can. I removed the bag in order to focus on exercise.

Breakfast was delayed until nine, after cleaning up a sink of dishes dirtied by sons making and eating brownies the night before. Cleaned bathroom before showering at ten thirty. Finally, at desk by eleven with tea and journal, breathing once or twice. At 11:05, Gray popped into my office to say goodbye before leaving for airport—a quick kiss, a "see ya, have fun," and he's gone. Worked half an hour until a robocaller shattered my concentration at noon. Since I was up, I grabbed a ten-minute lunch in the sunny kitchen. Ahhh. Uh oh, time to walk my dog, Bebe. Then, I figured I should assemble the chicken pot pie for dinner tonight. Ah, quiet! One boy is still sleeping, the other eating. I settle in at 2 p.m. for some serious writing. Where was I...?

Two minutes later, my cell phone rings. It's my mother, calling from McDonald's twenty minutes away. She and Dad are waiting for the road repair guy to arrive and jump-start their car. It could take 90 minutes--could I come pick her up? Of *course* I will. I hop in my trusty blue minivan, arrive at 2:25, just as the repairman is leaving. She takes the opportunity of the ride to my house to discuss what she wants to happen when she dies someday (though she is pretty hale at the moment). Apparently, she has decided to "visit" me often once settled on the "other side." "Don't worry," she says, "I won't be hanging out at the cemetery."

Home again, I struggle with the dog, put the TV on "*Dr. Oz*" and give Mom a magazine to read. My son Jack, 15, cooking buffalo chicken snacks in the oven, lets me know there is an annoying pop-up on TV he and Grandma can't dismiss. OK, back to my office. I grab a snack while catching up on *Late Show with Stephen Colbert* videos on YouTube. Brenin, 17, sneaks up on me, watches over my shoulder, yanks on the red curtains I use for "privacy" in my "dining room/office," puts my sticky notes on the ceiling. "Why don't I ever see you writing anything, Mom? You should get a real job."

Then Dad shows up, having bought his battery at the dealer. Defiant Dog jumps up, but Dad holds her back. My folks leave, I clean up, work for five more minutes. Then it's time to take Jack to school to pick up his tuba and suitcase from the band's Disney World trip. The sun breaks through the clouds, but rain continues to fall. I run to help, but my "little guy" has already hoisted everything into the back of the minivan.

A beautiful rainbow appears in the sky, guiding us home. Hallelujah moment!! Aaaahhh. "Mom! Eyes on the road!" Jack says. "Look at it later!"

As the pot pie cooks, Jack plays his tuba for 20 minutes—the entire repertoire, from *Tarzan* to *Star Wars*—and shows me his straw conical hat from China Pavilion at Epcot. At this point, after 6 p.m., I return to my desk and try to summon the joy I had felt that morning, the anticipation of a day of creation. It was gone. I give up and turn the computer off. It is not going to happen today.

I eat dinner, watch the college *Jeopardy* tournament with Brenin, and take the dog out. All ready for bed, I lie awake, the day's stories buzzing around in my head like flies at the screen window, straining to be let out. So, I grab my notebook and a pen, lock the bedroom door, and start writing. Hopefully, if I get it all out, I won't have that dream again where I desperately need to find the ladies' restroom but there are no stall doors, or they're all occupied.

I sense these stories may seem humorous in the future, but at this moment, I'm not laughing. It feels like my dreams are farther away than ever.

But are they, really? Who says?

PREFACE

Why do we women (especially in our middle years) put ourselves last so often?

Excuses abound. Yes, sometimes others really need our help. There will be a day when we miss these messy kids, once they have moved out, gone to college. Our parents won't live forever. The dog, too, has a limited life span (already 56 in people years). You always hear, "put yourself first." Yes, in terms of self-care that is essential. We need to be healthy and strong to be of any use to others. So, we eat right, hit the gym, sleep when we can, breathe. We do our hair and makeup, wear the right colors and accessories, and try to avoid looking like we belong in the three-way mirror on *What Not to Wear* with Clinton and Stacy shaking their heads and shouting, "Leslie, it's time to surrender the 'Mom jeans'!"

But what about shaking the dust from the wings of your dreams? You know those dreams--what you think about when you're ironing shirts and cleaning sinks, chauffeuring your kids, and walking the dog.

Dreams sneak up on you sometimes when you're listening to your husband talk excitedly about a new project at work, or your son tell you about the website he's creating for a class. It is a longing to create, to lose yourself in the "zone," like when Abba's "Dancing Queen" comes on and you're 11 again, disco roller skating with your friends. Then the song ends and you're standing in the middle of the kitchen floor covered in sweat, and the dog is tilting her head at you.

In my late thirties, I once told a "mom friend" after our sons' playdate, "You can have it all, maybe just not at the same time." At that moment, a little bell went off in my head. I think I had zeroed in on one of my life challenges, or lessons. And that, I think, was the moment I realized I *was* Zazoo Plazz, part-time superhero, full-time mom. She always lived in me, from birth, but this was an epiphany. It would take 10 to 12 more years for me to fully embrace her identity, but that was the start of my journey to create a successful life on my terms and define what *I* thought "having it all" meant.

Certainly, it didn't mean reaching some kind of perfection or world where nothing ever changed. I learned the hard way--that kind of idealism set me up for failure many times! I learned to embrace my quirkiness, laugh a bit more on the days when the planets clearly were not aligned in my favor. I began to collect my stories, and as I organized them, I started to see some patterns.

The funniest stories were the result of the times I took myself the most seriously and tried to do what I thought other people expected me to do or be who I thought I "should" be. In other words, the times when my expectations were through the roof, I set myself up for an "epic fail," as my kids used to say ("like, 5 years ago, Mom"). For example, rather than buy a small bag of crunchy kale chips for four dollars, I decided to devote an hour of my precious time to making three trays of kale chips from scratch. Is there any wonder they looked like the lawn after a hard rain and had the consistency of a rubber band?

If you are still reading this, I hope I've struck a chord (organ lesson stories to follow) and you realize we have something in common. At a minimum, I hope reading my stories will put a goofy smile on your face. But I *really* hope that you will read a passage that makes a little bell go off in your head and reminds you of your Dharma--what you are here to do. And you do it, bringing joy to yourself *and* the world. Then, you can check it off your soul's to-do list! Skip ahead two spaces and pick a card!

Now is the ideal time for all of us to rise to the challenge of feeling that familiar tug of war over our time, but forging ahead anyway, with baby steps. Communicating this message might be *my* divine purpose, since the sum of the letters in my name—Zazoo Plazz—is the Master Number '11,' the double 'masculine' one, referring to the self, creativity, and independence. Reduced to the 'feminine' two, this number finds purpose in nurturing and supporting people, and working together. I feel this pull constantly, and I suspect others—especially women—may feel it, as well.

There is a Zambian proverb that the "peeps" in my running club like to quote: "If you want to go fast, run alone; if you want to go far, run together." I love running a personal best time, shiny medals, and race shirts, as well as the adrenaline rush of crossing the finish line. But my best memories—and motivation—have come from running with, and in support of, other people. This is our time, our moment, to lace up our sneakers (unless you have those "no tie" performance laces, which save lots of time) and head off down our paths.

1

Hey, What's So Funny?

It must have been 1968 or 1969. I remember being about three or four, lying in my bed in the dark, listening to my parents laughing their heads off watching *Laugh-In* on a Friday night. My Dad has always had a hearty, unselfconscious cackle, which for the funniest skits would lead to guffawing and knee slapping. Is it any wonder I was curious? Eventually, they let me come in the den and squeeze onto the loveseat with them to watch a few minutes. The show was so colorful! The clothes, the set, and the jokes--the majority of which sailed over my head—were lively, fast-paced, and irreverent.

I was hooked. But the physical gags were the best!

To this day, I feel empowered remembering how Ruth Buzzi hit that white-haired guy with her big purse when he made lewd remarks to her.

But I think if my mother-in-law, with her ever-expanding collection of HUGE purses, ever hit a guy like that she might put him in the intensive care ward for a month.

In my black-and-white baby photo, I'm flashing a big toothless grin, my dark eyes glittering as if I am bursting to tell the punch lines to some great jokes you haven't yet heard. Maybe I was looking at Dad, because he always made me laugh. Freed from most of the mundane responsibilities shouldered by Mom—feeding, diapering, bathing, and educating—he happily spent his time with me goofing off in the most splendid ways.

I have a photo gallery in my mind of Dad sporting candy corn vampire teeth or orange slice grins, reading me the Sunday comics in the newspaper, vacuuming my orange bedroom carpet while wearing my blue high school cowboy hat, his lower lip twisted to the right and his brown glasses askew. He'd submerge in our above-ground pool and jump up like a swamp monster to make me squeal.

But as I grew older, I found that Dad was most skilled at puns—groan-worthy, perfectly timed phrases designed to boost the mood of any gathering (or send people running to their cars). Because he was so easygoing and mild-mannered, no one expected him to come out with some of these zingers. He listened, watched, and waited. We'd be listening to Mom's older brother, Uncle Moe, regale an audience with a story of a business conference he'd orchestrated in an exotic locale, and suddenly I'd see a sly grin creep across Dad's face. "Uh oh," I'd think, just before Dad would tiptoe into the conversation with a barb so brilliantly sarcastic it caused Moe to lose his place for a second while Dad smiled and absorbed the laughter.

In the 1970s, Dad let me watch some British comedy shows featuring "proper gentlemen" behaving in mischievous ways. Mom didn't care for the *Benny Hill Show*, maybe because it always ended with Benny playing tag around town with a bunch of scantily clad young women. I thought Dad liked hearing the show's theme song, because *he* played the saxophone, too. To this day, it's my "running around like a chicken with its head cut off" song when I have too much to do and not enough time, which is very often.

Far from corrupting me for life, Dad taught me how to relax and not take myself—or life—so seriously. More importantly, he taught me that laughing—and making others laugh—is healthy and noble, as long as no one gets hurt. And you can't please everyone. What is funny to one person might not be funny to someone else, and that's OK.

In second grade, I had a chirpy teacher who laughed from first thing in the morning until it was time to go home. To this day, I think of her only as "Laughing Lady." I love a good laugh, but learning is serious business. Some days "LL" was just too much for me (like the guy who worked out at my gym at six in the morning with cologne so strong I had to wear eucalyptus-scented ear buds up my nose just to get through my workout). One such day, I decided I needed a little break, so I wrote a note on my lunch napkin (in crayon) to excuse myself, to this effect: "Dear Mrs. X., please let Leslie go home. Love, Mommy." Is it any wonder she ever stopped laughing after she read my note long enough to call the principal (and my mother)?

Ultimately, I got permission to leave early that day, only because I was running a fever and shortly after came down with chicken pox--definitely *not* a laughing matter!

2

Nobody Puts Leslie in a Crib

In the finale of one of my favorite movies, *Dirty Dancing* (1987), Johnny Castle, the resort dance instructor played by Patrick Swayze, bursts into the auditorium during the final show and pulls Baby (Jennifer Grey) out of her hiding spot for the dance of a lifetime.

Twenty years earlier, I literally *was* a baby, stuck in my crib, trying desperately to join the action. I remember hearing the telltale trumpet riff that signaled the start of the *Dating Game*, Mom's favorite 1960s afternoon show. "Oh, she's having fun, without me!" was my reaction. I really wanted to see the contestants blow kisses to the audience! My retribution for being a baby who wouldn't let her mother get a break came thirty-five or so years later, with the birth of my second son, Jack, who ran at full speed all day and fell face-down whenever he happened to be when he ran out of steam.

Nobody Puts Leslie in a Crib

As a young child in the early 1970s, I remember many Saturday nights spent perched at the top of the stairs, eavesdropping, when my folks had company. I wondered if they were going to talk about me, or their kids, but usually they talked about grownup things like jobs, the news, and movies. I'd sneak down to the kitchen for a glass of milk and a cookie in my nightgown and pigtails but was promptly shooed back to the den to watch TV or tucked into bed, depending on the hour. Even in bed, I could smell the smoke from grownups' cigarettes and hear the clink of glasses and silverware. Everyone started out very polite and quiet, but usually by the end of the evening--after a few drinks--their voices rose, the men interrupted each other's stories, and the women started laughing a little louder.

Early on, I knew that entertainment was an important part of life for adults. Being around their friends and celebrating important occasions brightened their days. Just watching--or listening--to people having fun can make you feel good and guide you in creating your own merriment. Eight years after *Dirty Dancing* had me practicing my dance steps all summer in jean shorts and low white sneakers, Gray yanked me onto the dance floor and into a polka "cuddle" (which feels like playing Twister hopscotch™ on a moving walkway). Years later, we're still having fun—most of the time. But when my "fun meter" drops toward empty, I'll turn on our wedding party song, Sheryl Crow's "All I Wanna Do," start dancing, and—poof—it's 1995 again!

3

Bright Light

We mid-to-late 1960s babies arrived during a very energetic era, but could do little more than eat, sleep, and pick up the "groovy vibes" from our surroundings to interpret later in life. My parents brought me home from the hospital the week of November 9, 1965—just in time for the great Northeastern U.S. blackout to hit our Connecticut town. Reportedly, I slept through the entire blackout, as my poor parents were running around trying to heat up milk on the gas stove at my grandmother's house and rounding up candles and matches. When the lights blinked on, I woke up, smiled, and took my bottle as if nothing had happened. And nothing *had* happened—it got dark, which is why I went to sleep in the first place.

Bright Light

Having observed the rise and fall of party energy from an early age, I developed an instinct for social timing—knowing when to join the party and when to leave. But I was confused as to why some people seemed to stay at parties long past the time when I would have left. One weeknight we had some relatives over for dinner, after which the grownups sat around talking and finishing their coffee. At around 8 p.m., my bedtime, everyone was still there. I yawned a few times, but no one noticed. Finally, I got up and turned off the lights. Some people laughed heartily, but some definitely did not look amused. Is it any wonder my family is still speaking to me, after a stunt like that? I might have gotten away with it had I been a year or two younger. After first grade, I was a bit long in the tooth to look cute pulling stunts like this. People did get the hint and leave, though, so that method worked really well.

As I entered my pre-teen years, I realized electricity could be used in power-full ways. When I was reading in a room, Dad would come in and say, "How can you read in the dark?" and turn on a light, even if I didn't need it. Other times he'd get after me for leaving the lights *on* in a room. He set up timers to make the lights in our house go on at a certain time, so people would think we were home.

And when I was about 16, he surprised me and my boyfriend--as we arrived at my parents' Rhode Island beach cottage late one summer night--with a series of motion sensor lights positioned to blare directly into the car.

Is it any wonder that I married an electrical engineer?

4

Part-Time Private Eye

When Sting sang about someone watching "Every Breath You Take," he could have been referring to our neighbor, "Auntie" Ruth MacGreyhouse, who lived across the street from us when I was growing up. Mom and Dad had just built and moved into the green colonial with white shutters in 1963, and since the street was still quiet, had not yet hung drapes on the front bay window.

One evening, Mom caught sight of Auntie Ruth, ensconced in her parlor, training her binoculars on their first dinner party. The next day, and thereafter, there were white sheers and curtains on every inch of window facing the street.

They may have protected themselves from external surveillance, but my folks were still subject to constant scrutiny from *me*. I have boatloads of stories from my childhood, simply because my parents were just living their lives, probably not aware that I was recording everything they said and did in my little brain. I would often sit in the stairway and listen to my parents talk in the kitchen, not wanting to miss something important that I might need to know, like whether we were going out to dinner at Mr. Steak or Arthur Treacher's for fish and chips on Friday night (if it was the Lenten season and we couldn't eat meat on Fridays).

If I chimed in with an opinion ("fish and chips!"), my mother would whisper, "Gosh, that kid has good ears."

As an only child aspiring to a writing career, I quickly expanded my reporter's beat to include the immediate neighbors to each side and in back. Taking a page from my heroine, Harriet M. Welch (from *Harriet the Spy* by Louise Fitzhugh), I outfitted one of my dad's tool belts with a notebook, pen, and flashlight, and, in my cuffed jeans, low-top black sneakers, and sweatshirt, took off to spy on the neighborhood. Sometimes I used binoculars. I was never caught—at least I didn't think so.

Back then there were trees and fences everywhere, and lots of kids were playing outside, unsupervised.

My mother said, "Thank goodness, she's outside." "Come home for dinner!" was the only caveat. I'll always remember the Boston Italian mother in the Prince spaghetti commercial—aired in the New England states in the 1970s--calling her son "Anthony!" home for dinner: "On Wednesdays, he ran."

Harriet the Spy called to me around age seven or eight because I had been keeping a diary for a while and was fascinated with observing people and their daily activities. Mom spent $63 at the grocery store one week!

Like Harriet, I got to learn secrets, meet people, and record their names and the things they did at certain times. Sometimes I wrote short stories based on the people or pets I saw, and usually someone ended up being a ghost (thanks to my active imagination and too many hours spent reading Edgar Allen Poe and listening to Alfred Hitchcock records in the dark).

I preferred the world I created in my mind to the one adults lived in (and wanted me to enter someday). This early eavesdropping urge probably explains why I like to write facing a window, so I can see the neighbors come and go (just like Jimmy Stewart did in Alfred Hitchcock's 1954 thriller *Rear Window*, except without the gruesome plot line and the digging-in-the-backyard scene).

Without peering into windows, I accurately predict when people will walk their dogs, go to and return from work, and mow their lawns. I know whose house is for sale, and who came to look at it with a realtor. I know who hires a maid service and on which day they clean. I see who employs a lawn service and when they spray. It's pretty easy to draw conclusions about people based on these things, and hard to suspend judgment. I think this spying helped me to learn about the world around me, that things are not always what they seem, and that it pays to be patient and attentive, because something magical might happen at any time. I also realized that I had way more fun hanging back and watching, silently, than I did talking nonstop and "doing." My greatest achievements would likely come from the ability to "shape shift" into various disguises in order to discover things others don't know and share them with my community.

My knack for "getting to the bottom of things" explains my childhood obsession with the *Scooby-Doo Show* on Saturday mornings, and my identification with Velma, given my large glasses, orange turtleneck sweaters, and fondness for hearing the phrase uttered by villains unmasked on the show: "I would have gotten away with it, too, if it weren't for you meddling kids!"[2]

5

Pardon My French

All four of my grandparents were Franco-American (descended from Québécois, or Quebeckers, not Campbell's canned pasta company), but I learned the most "French" words from my mother's parents, whom I called Memere and Pepere. Later, when I took French in college and met some friends from Paris, I realized that over the 300-plus years our family had been out of France, trading furs and living in the wilds of Canada, they had gotten a little casual with the language and made up a few of their own colloquialisms. By the time I came along, my grandparents rarely spoke French, except when the Fall River, Massachusetts relatives came to visit—bearing bags of chow mein noodles--but a few French phrases often slipped into our conversations.

Along with the French phrases, Pepere was known to pepper his speech with a few expletives when things weren't going his way. One day when I was two years old, I announced to Mom's brother, Uncle Moe, and his wife, Bunny, that Pepere had taught me some French words. "Is that so?" they said. "Which ones?" I puffed up my chest, took a deep breath, and said "Son of a beech!" They laughed so hard their faces turned red, which confused me, because I didn't think I had made a joke. Pepere said that all the time! I thought it was a French word.

I took some liberties with French proper nouns, as well. Before I could say my full name, 'Leslie Bilodeau,' I would reply to all inquiries: "My name is Essie Bid-owe." It seemed like all the women in my mother's family had French nicknames, mostly based on food. My great-grandmother, whom I knew, briefly, as Big Memere, also went by "'ti chou," short for "mon petit chou," or "my little cabbage."

No doubt people intended "sweetheart," as "chou à la crème" means "cream puff." She gave me quarters, and had a nice, soft lap I could sit on when we visited her in the nursing home. Pepere used to call her Memere "ti poule," which is short for "petite poulet," or "little chicken." It sounded like "see pull" and aptly described Memere, who was short, thin, and small-boned. When Pepere—of stockier build—would find her chocolates hidden in a cigar box in the linen closet, she'd get mad and call him "Cochon!" (roughly, "you big, fat pig!"). Only Memere could call him that, and with as much feeling.

Memere called me "ma tannante," or "my little pest." I can't imagine how I earned that nickname, because I was always on my best behavior at her house. It was more fun to do dishes and make homemade lemonade in her kitchen, because it wasn't home, and you could soak up the ladies' conversation, which was way more fun than the "man talk" in the other room. Also, Memere had all kinds of antiquey jewelry, coins, and photos just waiting to be discovered in drawers and trap doors in the attic.

When I return to those childhood visits with Memere, she is smiling and teasing me, calling out, "Hey, ZaSu Pitts!" though I had no idea who, or what, a "Zazoo" (to my ears) might represent. But I was determined to get to the bottom of it someday. At first, I thought she called me Zazoo "Pitts" because I didn't like pits, in anything. If it had a stone, seed, or core, I needed to remove it--grapes, tomatoes, cherries, even cucumbers. It took me an hour to eat a slice of watermelon.

I also considered that "Zazoo Pitts" was a French term of endearment, like "ma tannante." I didn't ask Memere what it meant, or even wonder much about it, until I started collecting my stories, at which point I found my answer immediately in the annals of cyberspace. Za Su (Say-zoo) Pitts, short for Eliza Susan Pitts, was a popular film actress from Memere's day who made people laugh with her portrayals of jittery, nervous, wide-eyed, spinster busybodies like Gertie the switchboard operator in the comedy epic *It's a Mad, Mad, Mad, Mad World* (1963), and inspired the voice of Olive Oyl in *Popeye the Sailor* cartoons.[3]

But what impressed me most about Za Su was that she threw everyone for a loop by playing a tightfisted wife whose husband bites her fingers off because she won't give him any of her $5,000 lottery winnings in the 1924 silent tragedy *Greed*. The film's director/producer, Erich von Stroheim, called her "the greatest psychopathological actress in the American cinema" and that "she should not be in comedy, for she is the greatest of all tragediennes."[4] And she did all this without sound!

It appears that Ms. Pitts was an enigma—secretly smart, funny, intense, a bit loopy, and unpredictable. She must have made quite an impression, because she died two years before I was born and Memere saw her in me. I checked my fingers—whew, all there!

With this knowledge, I christened my inner child Zazoo "Plazz," short for my married name, "Placzek." Zazoo liked to go off by herself sometimes and imagine all the fun she was going to have someday. She was the mischievous, curious, creative Little Leslie that went off exploring, imagining, dancing, and having audacious adventures when people were—and were not--watching. I was the kid who kept her parents on their toes and her relatives in stitches—laughing, that is. I may have been bored at times, but no one could ever say that I was boring.

Stay tuned for more Zazoo adventures!

6

Going With the Flow

My mother was a Master multitasker, before they coined that phrase, and she passed that down to me. Every morning after breakfast when I was about two, she stationed me on the little potty chair in the dining room next to a tall stack of books and let me go at it, so she could get some things done around the house. She had probably put a load of laundry in the washing machine and was talking on the phone or brushing her teeth while listening to the news on the radio. This was a win-win for both of us: alone time to nourish our minds while listening to the soothing sounds of running water.

I've done some of my best thinking on the potty, and this habit has followed me into adulthood, with radical results.

Just last week I was thinking about starting a new movement. The ability to carve out some "me time" in the bathroom really came in handy when my boys were small. After a particularly exhausting day, I would grab any handy reading material--like *Lego* magazine or Gray's *IEEE Spectrum*—and head for the bathroom, lock the door, and relish five or ten minutes alone. I realized my bathroom is a perfect place to write—there's plenty of paper, and a window for fresh air and inspiration.

Should an urge arise to multitask, I can swish my mouth and meditate while painting my toes.

My mother's decision to hone my self-control while instilling in me a love of reading was not merely an exercise in convenience. As an avid reader with a fascination in New Age or "counterculture" subjects such as astrology, she knew I was a Scorpio, a fixed water sign for whom "still waters run deep." In other words, there was a lot going on below my calm, stable demeanor. To prepare me for my childhood yoga practice, she likely wanted to fast-track my chakra development, revving up the bottom three (grounding, creativity, and learning) to allow me to focus on the higher, more spiritual chakras by age seven or eight.

On a physical level, I learned that energy (food) that goes in at one end comes out the other, in one way or another.

At the same time, ideas from the books I "consumed" wormed their way into my receptive brain and re-entered the world as "Zazoo purges" of poems, exclamations, drawings, and adventures.

Voracious for new ideas, I read most of the books in the children's section of our town's library by second grade—even the biographies--and moved on to the densely packed, three-level labyrinth where the grown-up books awaited discovery. I was overjoyed to see that I had a long way to go before I ran out of reading material, and the chairs were so comfortable! Sometimes I would hide in the upper level stacks for hours and sit on the floor, my feet propped up on a bookshelf, or wedge myself in a corner by the staircase, where I couldn't easily be found or asked to move.

Recently, out of curiosity, I did a search on "potty chairs" and was amazed to see that one of those stores where you can buy towels, toasters, and monogrammed nose hair clippers offered a potty chair with an iPad™ attached.[5] Undoubtedly, this "potty Pad" was the talk of the baby shower, but I couldn't help but feel nostalgic for my sons' little plastic chair, in between my own and this futuristic one. We spent a hot August weekend in 2003 "cramming" potty training in before my oldest son went off to preschool.

Following a book's advice, we let him run around sans shorts all weekend and showed him a video of a little boy his age exploring the far reaches of space and the ocean on his potty-mobile.[6] He was so mesmerized by the video, he left the diapers behind for good. I don't remember training my younger son—he may have trained himself, trying to keep up with his older brother. In any case, I spared my son the embarrassment of taking pictures of this stage, preferring to take mental snapshots instead. But my mother did not subscribe to that way of thinking.

Once, to my horror, Mom showed a photo of me on my "thinking chair" to a high school boyfriend. Gazing now at my curly brown mop flopping in my eyes as I clasped a book featuring well-dressed bunnies over my bare, chubby legs, I give thanks—once again--that we didn't have social media back in those days. (Photo next page).

Leslie B. Placzek / Adventures of Zazoo Plazz

Zazoo on her "thinking chair."

7

Don't Eat the Toothpicks!

The first time I went over to my husband Gray's apartment after we started dating, in July, 1994, I noticed a strange note taped to his kitchen message board: "DON'T EAT THE TOOTHPICKS!" My first reaction was, "Oh no, what are we dealing with here?" because I'd seen relationships end after these sorts of omens popped up in my face. But this guy was different—he seemed to "get" my view of the universe.

So, I asked him what the note meant. He said, "Oh, that's from my mom. She always tapes that note to her cupcakes."

To illustrate, he grabbed a paper plate of cupcakes sitting on the counter, frosting quickly dissolving despite the air conditioning. I saw that toothpicks had been stabbed randomly into the helpless desserts, which were straining to breathe under layers of plastic wrap like a bridesmaid trying sweat off ten pounds before the wedding with a "Weight loss miracle tip! No exercise necessary." "You keep that note up there so you won't forget and accidentally eat a toothpick?" I asked. "You got it," he said.

He put down the cupcakes and licked frosting from his hands. Suddenly, it dawned on me that I had found a guy who would maintain his sense of humor despite any obstacles life might toss his way, as he had stuck that silly note to his wall amidst unpaid bills, letters and photos of relatives and friends, "Dilbert"[7] cartoons, and a prominent picture of himself sitting in his "single guy" car (a fiery red 1991 Acura Integra RS with two spacious front seats and a hatchback for a couple of duffel bags and beach chairs).

Over the years, I've come to expect my mother-in-law to do things the "old school" way, with a twist. Maybe she'd learned them from *her* mom, or sister. Follow the recipe, include some love, and for goodness' sake, at least *try* to keep them looking edible until they reached their destination, were acknowledged, and eaten. It's the thought that counts, anyway. Therein lies the essence of "Mom P.," as I call her—she has "other stuff" to do, people to see, stores to shop.

I found her philosophy refreshing, if confusing. I was accustomed to the perfect symmetry of my mom's cupcakes, spaced two fingers apart, the frosting a perfect sphere ending precisely one centimeter from the fluted edges of the pastel or foil liner, with a jellybean on top at Easter. They were too beautiful to eat. Had Instagram existed in the 1970s, I would have posted them. I feared spoiling the effect--should I take this one, or the other? Mom's cakes traveled in a special Tupperware™ tote. I don't recall her using toothpicks, except to test if bread was done or to serve Swedish meatballs or cheese cubes. The picks stood in their own little cylinder, *adjacent* to the food.

On the rare occasion I make cupcakes, they fall somewhere in the middle. If I'm in a hurry, the frosting might be laid on a little thicker on some cupcakes than others, and the sprinkles tossed rather than placed. If I drop one on the floor, the dog (or a boy) likely cleans it up. Eventually they look pretty good, and I serve them in a carrier or on one of those metal towers. They usually disappear quickly, unless I make the "healthy" version.

Like Mom, I keep my toothpicks locked up at home. I don't want to accidentally drop them all over the floor, since I wouldn't be able to count them by sight, as did Raymond Babbitt (played by Dustin Hoffman), well-meaning savant and older brother of Charlie Babbitt (Tom Cruise) in the "Pancake Tuesday" scene of the 1988 movie *Rainman*, and I'd be finding them under the stove for years to come.

After we were married, Mom P. bought me a plastic toothpick dispenser she'd seen advertised on TV,[8] sold alongside other useful gadgets like microwavable egg molds and wraparound sunglasses. When one pushes down on the red bird perched on top, he bends over and picks up a toothpick in his beak from a secret, sliding compartment. Cocktail parties would never be the same.

8

Part-time Passion for Fashion

One spring day, I showered and threw on some stretchy navy cropped pants, my favorite lilac buttoned-down shirt, no-show socks, and running sneakers. With some small silver earrings, a swipe of concealer and blush, I was ready for anything the day might throw at me. My 15-year-old son looked up from his phone, glanced at me, and said, "Mom. You look like a man." Then, he resumed texting. This snarky teenage observation prompted me to figure out what he meant. Did I forget to draw on my eyebrows today?

I squinted into the hall mirror, and there "it" was. With my curly brown pixie cut, I was channeling "Pat,"[9] Julia Sweeney's early-1990s *Saturday Night Live* character of uncertain gender (but taller, and not as thick in the torso).

Ewwww! I slathered on some lilac lipstick, loosened one shirt button and switched to flats. Better. But I have to admit that there is a "managerial" air about me. Donning a shirt with buttons and some wash-and-wear pants drives home the message: "I mean business." I intimidated my own child. Heels might have softened the look, but I spend half of my day writing in my home office, and the other half walking the dog, cleaning, cooking, running errands, and doing laundry. I need comfortable footwear.

Mom P., who stopped working in the mid-to-late 1960s when pregnant with her only child, my husband, calls herself a "domestic engineer." I always reply, "Not me. I'm management." We're both cleaning the bathroom, but the difference is that I *look* like I could run out to meet a client at any moment--and I'd be ready. I tell her this, but she still gives me aprons, probably in the hope that I'll become more domestic. Last year for Christmas she gave me a black and white apron with red ruffles and roosters. I save it for when I want to dress up as (1950s-'60s TV mom) June Cleaver[10] for Halloween.

Leslie B. Placzek / Adventures of Zazoo Plazz

Part-time Passion for Fashion

Until recently, two types of clothing held sway over my wardrobe: work clothes and exercise clothes. Because my part-time jobs did not create sufficient income or incentive to gussy myself up, I had let that part of my wardrobe drift as my initial enthusiasm for those jobs waned.

I had some pants, blouses, and sweaters that felt cool, perky, and fresh a few years ago, but now--not so much. Kind of like me!

At the same time, I worked out every day and ran races. Every time I went in a clothing store, I would start off in the regular women's clothing section, become restless, and then leap over to the active section, where I'd inevitably find a new tee shirt declaring "You Got This" or "Free Your Mind." Sometimes I'd get new socks, cropped tights or shorts. My workout drawer was stuffed with race jerseys and swishy track pants. The other drawers held pajamas and lounge pants--heaven!

Shoved in the back of the closet were the "special" items--a bright party dress I'd worn to my father's 80th birthday party, my beloved purple "Easter egg" dress, a cool green and white polka dot sleeveless dress I'd worn to an environmental awards dinner for work two years ago, and a black "moto" jacket I deemed too racy for church and work and most other places I frequent with my husband. I wondered why I had bought it, been so impractical.

The shoes were in proportion to the clothes--thirty percent practical heels and flats, sixty percent running shoes and casual sandals or slippers, and ten percent dressy heels and boots. There was a pair of sparkly black satin pumps I wore to an office holiday party six years ago, before budget concerns did away with holiday parties. I wondered why I kept the black suede booties with heels too high to walk in comfortably.

You could say that my closet reflected my life--surviving the workday, living to work out, and occasionally stepping out for a party or date. I realized that I had very few "in between" occasion clothes anymore--clothes to wear on adventures. Perhaps society had become more casual in the past twenty years while I was buying baby and boy clothes, men's work shirts, gifts for parents and friends. I wore my work clothes to school and church events, and workout clothes or jeans for everything else.

Shopping for myself made me feel like I was wasting time and money. I drifted back and forth between the stores where my mother shops and the minimalist "capsule wardrobes" dotting my Pinterest feed, like a spirit trapped in a pinball machine, never really coming to rest on "my look."

When Mom P. fancied a night off from cooking, and someone asked, "What's for dinner?" she'd say, "whatever falls out of the freezer." When in a hurry or in doubt, I'll wear "whatever falls out of the closet." I crave a uniform, like I wore for eight years of Catholic school: white blouses; solid, neutral skirts or pants; and a little "flair" from a special scarf, sweater, or necklace. Freed from the daily tether of outfit indecision, I have an abundance of creative energy to expend on my most enticing projects. Sometimes I get lucky and find items online that scream "This is Leslie!" like the black and white "Do Not Disturb" floppy hat meant for the beach that now guards the entrance to my home office.

Uniforms support me when I'm showing up fully for life. The summer before my freshman year in college, I waitressed at the "Chickadee" sandwich shop at the Rhode Island shore dressed in white cargo pants, white sneakers, a red golf shirt and a neat belt, my hair in a bun or braid. Every night I came home smelling like a fryer, washed my clothes in the tub, and put them back on the next day. I met my husband, Gray, while working in a food tent on a golf course, dressed in khaki shorts, a navy "Greater

Hartford Open" golf shirt, no makeup, and a ponytail. He claimed to love my "au naturel" look—even *after* he saw me in the fancy white dress.

I came to see that my sartorial souring came to pass because I defaulted to supporting others' dreams and passions at the expense of my own. New paths, new friends, and fresh adventures will attract pin-worthy outfits and accessories, and maybe I'll shrug off some of those adverse astrological aspects between "Venus" (the planet, not the 1986 Bananarama song by that name) and the rest of my chart. And I'll stop having those dreams where I can't go out because I can't find anything to wear in closets filled with little-girl jumpsuits, Robert-Palmer-girl[11] black dresses, and polyester pants with "comfort" waists like they used to advertise in Sunday newspaper circulars. I'll prepare to laugh when a salesperson asks if they can "help" me "find something."

I've accepted that my style is ideally suited to a woman with two sons, married to an Eagle Scout, who liked to take Skipper[12] camping among the pine trees as a child rather than drive Barbie around in a pink convertible. I no longer apologize for the glee I experience at trying on a new, black, fully adjustable stretchy belt with an interlocking snap in the front, even while a snarky teenager asks me when my shift starts at the local home improvement superstore. I can't wait for the slinky silver belt to arrive.

9

Kitchen Explorations

Every now and then I get bored with my cooking or feel like I've plateaued in my quest to maximize my health, and I get inspired by a book, website, or food celebrity to "BAM! Kick it up a notch,"[13] as Chef Emeril Lagasse likes to say. So, instead of trying one or two dishes and calling it a day, as my mom would do, I overhaul everything and turn the household upside down. That is what happened one winter.

On February 20th--a date forever etched in the memory of all five of my senses--I made paleo shepherd's pie with grass fed ground lamb tempted by the nutritionist's equivalent of the snake in the Garden of Eden. I am going to pay for that one for a long time. I'm not sure if my son, Jack, was more disappointed that I used "counterfeit mashed potatoes" (also known as whipped cauliflower) on top, or that the lamb was so pungent we had to dump the casserole outside.

It took half a bottle of lemon juice in vinegar to get the smell out of the house. To Jack's credit, he took a bite of lamb before asking if the local sandwich shop was still open.

Having been largely lamb-deprived as a child (and objecting to eating innocent, fluffy, white animals, as a rule, even before I saw Anthony Hopkins and Jodie Foster in *The Silence of the Lambs*), I assumed that the strong smell owed more to the "lamb" than the "grass fed" characteristic of the meat. One evening in late April, I realized the error of this assumption when I attempted to concoct our family favorite, lasagna, with grass fed ground beef. Upon removing the meat from the package, I gagged on the smell, threw the meat in the trash and channeled Clara Peller-- the white-haired, diminutive spitfire in the blue dress in Wendy's 1984 commercial—with her ubiquitous catchphrase: "Where's the beef?"[14] I was crumbling a few thawed regular patties I'd found in the freezer into a frying pan when Jack came in after a Boy Scout meeting and said, "It smells like butt crack in here."

Snacks were my last chance to add to my nutritional repertoire, and—or so I thought—a slam dunk.

One March, my latest food guru suggested I toast up some seaweed with oil and sea salt for a tasty bite. I filed this one under: "Food that's really good for you, but life's too short to eat it—really?!" First of all, I had never used "tasty" and "seaweed" in the same sentence before. Usually I spend half the day at the beach trying to unwind the seaweed from my legs, and now you want me to eat it on purpose, and pay for it?

Later that month, I thought it would be a great idea to cook up some "crunchy kale chips," as they were described, leading to what I now call "The Great Kale Fail." As a rule, I'll throw kale in a soup with some beans and sausage, blanch the heck out of it, and eat it with some nice woven cracker points, a generous sprinkle of Parmesan cheese, and maybe a glass of white Zinfandel. It took me nearly an hour to piece, wash, and dry the little curly kale pieces. Ideally, I would have melted the coconut oil first, poured it over the kale, and then thrown in salt and coconut flour before toasting it to perfection on a cookie sheet in the oven. But the cold chunks of coconut oil clumped on the kale so the flour stuck only in spots--I had to keep patting the flour on the kale and tossing it like a salad. After it crisped in the oven and scented the kitchen like tropical oil

Kitchen Explorations

(the kind we used in the 1970s to get a deep tan), I put them in a plastic container to enjoy later. When I opened the container the next day, I found a bed of limp, chewy, flour-encrusted green clumps similar to the garnishes served--only for show--on the plate at fancy restaurants. I popped one in my mouth and chewed for about ten minutes, finally giving up and spitting it into the trash. I grabbed some red grapes and nuts and threw the kale out to compost in the woods with last year's Halloween pumpkin.

I chalked up the winter food fails to Lenten sacrifices taken to the extreme and incorporated a few new healthy ingredients—like gluten-free pasta—into our regular meals. Food optimist that I am, I was back at it a month later, carefully rinsing out mung beans in a jar with a fancy plastic cover guaranteed to produce "full grown, delicious sprouts" for my springtime salads. After a week I moved them to a cookie sheet with a damp cloth over them, as instructed, only to find them looking like what my dog deposits on the rug when she doesn't get her heartworm "treat." I paid my respects to the "mung bean massacre" before tossing it into the growing compost pile. "Mom," asked Jack, "why do you want to eat dung beans, anyway?"

10

As I Sew, So Shall I Weep

From the Letter of St. Paul to the Galatians, New Testament of the Bible:

"Bear one another's burdens and so you will fulfill the law of Christ. Make no mistake... the one who sows for the spirit will reap eternal life from the spirit. Let us not grow tired of doing good, for in due time we shall reap our harvest, if we do not give up."[15]

Inspired by the Bible passage above, I decided to do something nice for my husband one year for his March birthday. Somehow he had torn the back of the arm, near the cuff, of his favorite teal and white-striped button-down work shirt. I wore out my fingers searching high and low online but could not find a similar shirt. I also struck out at the "name-brand discount store" around the corner.

As I Sew, So Shall I Reap

The golden rule seems to be—buy long sleeves in the summer, short sleeves in the winter.

Out of options, I decided to fix it myself, though the fabric was frayed. With nothing to stitch onto, I ended up pinching the fabric together in something resembling an arm-pleat. It reminded me of a dirndl skirt I had in the early 1980s--with buttons down the front and rickrack around the hem, I could have worn it to serve beer at Oktoberfest, had I been of legal drinking age at that time.

I worked on that sleeve for almost an hour and at the end I was ready to throw the dang shirt and the sewing basket out the window. Finally, I cut the thread, said "good enough," and shoved the shirt back in the closet. "Maybe he won't wear it until next year," I thought. "I hope he can get his arm through the opening." A week later, I saw him wearing the shirt. He had removed my awkward arm-pleat and inserted a few barely visible stitches around a neat swatch of material cut from the hem. I wanted my hour back.

This little story illustrates why Gray is the master seamster (or tailor) in our house, sewing on Scout badges and making everything from curtains to tablecloths. Somehow, I am missing the sewing gene that was so bountifully bestowed upon my dad's mom, Granny, who used to make custom ball gowns for rich people back in the 1920s through the 1950s, as well as colorful afghans (throws) for me and my cousins. Until her eyes started to fail, she was an adept knitter, crocheter, and seamstress. I was OK at making small afghans--like the one with the red, white, and blue squares I made for the 1976 Bicentennial celebration—but anything more complicated caused me to get frustrated and start throwing things.

Likely hoping that I'd save money by whipping up my own curtains and linens, Gray bought me a sewing machine when we moved into our new house in 1997. It was gold, with a little pedal you pushed to speed it up, like a car accelerator. First, I tried to make simple green-checked curtains for the living room. He set me up in the spare bedroom with the threaded machine and material and let me go at it. He heard "Whirrrrrrr—sh*t! Whirrrrrrrrr-sh*t!" several times, then came to my rescue. I jumped for joy when a curtain shop opened within five miles of our house.

Maybe if I had stuck with it, as the Galatians verse says, I would have reaped my harvest. In fact, I can do a mean pants hem. My mom also had a sewing machine and made a lot of my clothes when I was a kid--mother-daughter dresses, Halloween costumes, and dance recital leotards. Her machine sat in the small, well-lit alcove off her bedroom where she applied her makeup. Mom was endlessly patient, until she got tired and had to take a break. It's a good thing that I had boys; I don't think even Gray would have had the temperament to sew five hundred red sequins onto a black leotard for the "jazzy tap" number.

In the 1970s and '80s, Mom belonged to a "craft club" which met every week or two at different ladies' houses to work on projects. It seemed to me, though, that it was just an excuse to have dessert and coffee and yack about goings-on in our parish, school, or neighborhood. Even if she wasn't really working on anything, she'd go and pretend to be fixing a shirt or something, just to hear all the good dirt. But she always came home happy from craft club, so I guess it was a good thing.

11

It Just Makes Scents

"Perfume is like a parenthesis, a moment of freedom, peace, love and sensuality in between the disturbances of modern living."-
Sonia Rykiel

As a young teen in the late 1970s and early '80s, I was fascinated by television commercials--perhaps more so than by the shows which they interrupted—because they were, at that time, memorable *and* entertaining, if a bit cheesy and predictable.

To this day, I can still picture the woman in the fancy suit, hair, and heels in the Enjoli[16] perfume commercial tossing her briefcase aside as she sashays through the door, singing in a sultry voice about bringing home the bacon. In the 1982 version, she riffles through a thick stack of dollar bills and clutches them tightly in her raised fist as if doing karate, her gaze fixed straight ahead.

She looks like she is going to punch anyone who stands in her way. What a power trip—she was a real superhero, Mom and Dad rolled into one!

It did not occur to me until I was in my 40s that the commercial made no allowance for how tired a "real" woman could be after working all day, cooking dinner, and cleaning up—especially if she has children! All we know of "Enjoli™ man" is that he offers to make dinner "for the kids" while she is reading them bedtime stories. What a guy! He's probably been reading the paper on the couch for the last half hour with his shoes off and tie loosened, five o'clock shadow on his face and cold drink in hand. Meanwhile, she still looks flawless—not a hair out of place--and smells like a bouquet of orchids, even after frying bacon and toughing out rush-hour traffic in the city. She'll need at least three or four sprays of perfume to spice up her 24-hour life, assuming she still wants to smell good in bed.

The name "Enjoli"[17] roughly means "pretty" (from the French "jolie"), and is a portmanteau,[18] or blend, of the words "enjoy life."   I wondered when the woman got to do that—before she cooked the bacon and made it to work for "five of nine," or after work and before "Tickety-tock" time? It seemed to me that she was a smart, caring person dedicated to serving and supporting others, and that lovely magical potion she sprayed on her neck was possibly the only nice thing she did *just for herself* all day. And who, I wondered, enjoyed life the most in this whole scenario? Was it the woman herself, her coworkers, or her family? And which cologne did the 24-hour man wear, if he existed?

I don't remember wanting to *be* the "Enjoli" lady (let's call her "Jolly"), nor did I know anyone like her at the time. But she got me thinking about how to remain true to myself, to keep that magic in my life, while serving others in the grown-up roles of career woman, wife, and mother.

At first glance, Jolly and I have little in common: I prefer sleeping in lounge pants and tee shirts to silky negligees; I'd rather wear jeans and a sweater than a skin-tight dress on a date; and I'd be grumpy if forced to wear a suit, blouse, stockings, and heels all day. And best of all, my husband cooks the bacon—turkey and regular--on weekends, with the blueberry pancakes.

Yet, I can relate to the difficulty of shifting from work mode to parenting mode, of remaining fully present and focused on what is most important. Often, I would be still at work in my head while physically at home or arrive at work and be thinking about whether the dog went out, if I'd signed a field trip permission slip, or how I'd snapped at my husband on the way out the door. Working remotely--21st-century-style--has created actual 24-hour women (and men). Scent—especially one with layers that appear as the day unfolds—helps us to breathe, smile, and put things in perspective.

I now understand why Jolly pressed her briefcase, pan, or hand to one hip while brandishing the perfume bottle in front of her like a can of pepper spray: it is her shield. Once a woman sprays her signature scent on her neck, her wrists, behind her ears, she reminds herself—and everyone she meets—that she is unique and magical, even as she is preparing yet another slide presentation, making the kids' peanut butter and jelly sandwiches, or massaging her husband's tight shoulders as he talks about his day. Each moment, each memory, takes up space in the brain with the scent molecules, labeled "wife" or "mom" and lingers long after they are gone.

The blind, retired Army Lt. Colonel Frank Slade, played by Al Pacino in the 1992 movie *Scent of a Woman*, relied on his acute sense of smell to identify the qualities of three different women by the perfume they were wearing.

That scene was a lot more romantic than the one in a recent pain cream commercial, where an elderly lady approaches a young woman wearing exercise clothes in the produce aisle of the supermarket and tells her she smells "just like my Walter (her late husband)."[19] No one wants to smell like "Walter," even if he *was* a 24-hour man.

12

Zazoo's Pen Plazz

*Dedicated to the memory of
"Captain Keyboard."
Daryl Dragon (1942-2019)*

When I was ten, I fell in love with the Captain and Tennille, a husband-and-wife duo enjoying peak popularity for unforgettable pop songs such as "Love Will Keep Us Together," "Do That to Me One More Time," and that mosh pit single, "Muskrat Love." I especially admired Daryl Dragon, who had played keyboards for the Beach Boys and really looked dapper in a ship captain's hat. He reminded me of my dad, who was also musical and quiet. I was mesmerized by Toni Tennille's wide smile, halo of hair, and soothing voice. They were like the cool aunt and uncle I wanted to visit.

I imagined we'd all play keyboards and sing—while wearing our turtlenecks –then cuddle with their bulldogs in front of the fire. I had all their albums and played some of their songs on the organ, so the next logical step was to write them a fan letter and join their pen pal club.

Upon enrolling in the Captain and Tennille fan club, I received an autographed photo of the happy couple, and a members' list of fans in my age group. How exciting! I grabbed my Bic™ four-color pen and Snoopy writing paper and started writing. Within a week or so, I was receiving envelopes addressed to me in chubby cursive--sometimes sporting a puppy or kitten sticker--and postmarked Ohio, Nevada, and California. I carried my letters out to the orange picnic table on the wood-paneled screened-in porch and laid them all out, pored over each one carefully, and considered my responses.

As I read the letters and looked at the girls' photos, I became aware of how simple and boring my life seemed in comparison, with no siblings, pets, or unusual hobbies to report. So, where my real life fell short, I used my imagination. Using the *Brady Bunch* TV show as my reference point, I told one girl I had an older brother, others that I had a big dog or a station wagon—then added some true elements, such as trips to the Rhode Island shore or

Cape Cod, Massachusetts. A problem arose: I had to make a table of my lies to each person so I could perpetuate the fantasies. It finally got to be too much, forcing me to stop lying and go to confession. What if the nuns found out?

I did keep one pen pal: Erica Fizzledak from Ohio. I never lied to Erica, which probably explains why we remained pen pals for over 40 years. We wrote to each other through high school and college, jobs and boyfriends, my marriage and kids, her caring for ailing parents. We sent pictures of each other's dogs—her Spots, my Bebe--and exchanged birthday cards each November. But two years ago, my Christmas card went unreciprocated. She rarely returned my e-mails and resisted the lure of social media. I had hoped we were going for 50 years--and that we would meet someday, maybe even post a video of ourselves on the "C & T" Facebook page!

Around the time we fell out of touch, I was crushed to hear that love had not kept them together after all—Toni Tennille had filed for divorce from the Captain in 2014, after 39 years. A message on their fan page explained that "Toni and Daryl have…put their 'Official…Fan Club' on hold until further notice." I wondered, "Was this my fault, because I stopped playing the organ, and replaced their poster with the Andy Gibb one? Did I need to go to confession again?" Perhaps Erica was meant to exist only as long as my childhood icons kept up the façade. In any case, having a pen pal was an opportunity to teach my boys about the satisfaction that comes from having lasting relationships—and, of course, where to put the stamp on an envelope.

13

Next Life Savings and Loan

*"If you would indeed behold the spirit of death, open your heart
wide unto the body of life.
For life and death are one, even as the river and the sea are one."*
Kahlil Gibran, *"On Death,"*
The Prophet

I have always loved dressing up and strutting around on Halloween night—the more extreme the costume, the better. I'd make my way down my dark street, trying not to gawk at the shadows darting to my right and left. In the few blocks where my parents permitted me to trick-or-treat, most kids made a bee line for the homes judged to be best-decorated, brightest lit, and where one would receive the biggest candy payout. With good reason, we avoided completely dark houses—no one was home, or maybe they were inhabited by witches with gnarled hands, waiting to lure children to their lairs with tainted candy.

But I always scratched my head over the houses where someone was clearly home—car in driveway, TV flashing in the living room—yet no outside light beckoned children to their door at seven in the evening. Were they unaware it was Halloween? Had someone eaten all their candy and they were unable to get to the store to buy more? I wanted to ring their doorbells--despite my parents' warnings against it--and ask, "What's the deal with you people?" I likened it to being Ebenezer Scrooge[20] ("Boo humbug!") or not believing in the Great Pumpkin.[21] The uncertainty frightened me more than any ghoulish costume, cold-blooded movie scream, or even the time I nearly drowned bobbing for the last apple in the vat at Leifa Tracter's combination Halloween/birthday party.

Two days later, when the air had become crisper, the trees more naked, and the wind somewhat harsher, I celebrated my birthday on the Day of All Souls. It was one big Zazoo party—with a day in between to reflect and go to the All Saints Day Mass and pray for all the people who passed away in the previous year.

I sensed a hierarchy, even as a child. The innocents, martyrs, and saints revered on November 1st were good as gold and now held "FastPasses"[22] to heaven (no lines, no waiting), the "end of the line" tortured ghouls speeding down the grease-slicked "Highway to Hell" (the ones I imagined AC/DC sang about in the rock song by that name). The ones who needed our help—you guessed it—were in the *middle* of the line. **BOO!**

If November 1st fell on a Saturday, I could "trick-or-treat" on Friday night, drop all the collection envelopes for the dead (as well as the weekly and monthly envelopes) in the basket at Saturday Vigil Mass, then, if I had any money left, celebrate my birthday the rest of the weekend with a clear conscience.

I usually wrote the names of everyone I could remember who died in the past year on the All Souls Day envelope, and if I still had room, I put my grandparents on there, even though they died a long time ago. One year I realized I had been paying (and praying) for my husband's cousin's great aunt Gladys for fifteen years and I'd only met her once.

I wonder what the statute of limitations is on praying for souls. If someone graduates from Purgatory, can they give their surplus prayers to someone else? Maybe they could stash my extra prayers in a CAP account (Credits against Purgatory) for my future use. In any case, plagued by the thought that I've left someone important out of my intentions, I say a general catch-all prayer every day for "all the souls," like the sweeping "for all my sins" in the confessional.

As a Scorpio, a fixed water astrological sign for whom nearly everything is black and white, yin and yang, wrong or right, I've always struggled with philosophical grey areas. I imagine that sitting in heaven's waiting room may be like standing in a long line for the sole ladies' room at a rock concert, regretting that large soda I just drank. Ow! Another scenario involves submitting a resume for a job posted online—along with a thousand other people—and waiting patiently for a response. "Well? Will I get an interview, or not?" This kind of uncertainty leads to merciless navel gazing. You might be uncomfortable, but at least you'd have plenty of company.

Since I've received so many good wishes and blessings on my birthday, I've always felt an obligation to remind folks of the day's significance. I told my husband-to-be, "I was born on the day of the dead!" on our first date, but that didn't scare him off at all.

Each November I bring out the "Catrinas," modern symbols of death used in the three-day celebration Mexicans call "Día de los Muertos," or "Day of the Dead."[23] A friend gave me a "sugar skull" ornament--boasting cheek curlicues, eye socket petals, and forehead flowers—after I admired her Catrina-themed running skirt. It warms my heart to think that the souls of the beloved departed are invited back for an annual visit, and their lives celebrated with food, festivities, and humor. Death comes for all, even for "La Calavera Catrina,"[24] the iconic high-society skeleton in the big hat and fancy dress popularized by early-twentieth-century Mexican artists.

14

Perplexed Planetary Pupil

As far back as I can remember, my mother was an amateur astrologer. She didn't look at the night sky, but she analyzed people's date, time, and place of birth and produced eerily exact portraits of their personality, motives, and destinies. When I was growing up, Mom always had her blue, dog-eared copy of the *New York Times* Best Seller-listed *Linda Goodman's Sun Signs* (1968), a bible for aspiring astrologers, (and its red-hot sequel, *Love Signs (1978)*) on her bedside table, as well as the *Dell Horoscope* magazine, pencils, and notebooks. There was a crucifix on the wall next to her bed, and a little altar with angel figurines, crystals, a rosary, little books for meditation, and a chime. She would sit in bed many nights after dinner—doors closed--and pore over her manuals like a granddad in the outhouse with the *Old Farmer's Almanac*.

Perplexed Planetary Pupil

I sensed as a child that Mom studied this "secret" science to tell people things they wanted to hear about themselves or others. She had this way of acting like she "knew" things, and if you asked for an explanation she would tell you just so much, and then close her eyes, as if it was too taxing to try to explain any more to the "uninitiated." Sigh.

A few times I peeked at her books when she was otherwise occupied, but it was such a maze of charts and funny-looking symbols I quickly grew discouraged. I lacked the patience to learn her craft, so I was limited to asking her specific questions, which as I became a teenager and adult was increasingly awkward. I knew all about my sun sign, Scorpio, from the Sydney Omarr[25] paperbacks in my bookcase, but soon came to learn that astrology went far beyond the sweeping horoscope most people read in the newspaper.

Mom had told me that to really do a person's chart, or get to the juicy details, you needed to know the specific time and place they were born. And you can't just walk up to someone and ask them, "Oh, by the way, what time were you born?" After which you could gasp, "Oh, no! Not 4 a.m.! That gives you Leo rising! Darn, I was hoping we could be friends, but I just don't get along with Leos."

Likely, I struck out with the "What's your sign" pickup line in middle school more often than the bell-bottomed, platform-heeled disco crowd.

I always wondered how you could tell someone, "Uranus conjuncts your ascendant" with a straight face. (Later I learned that the proper pronunciation was "YER-uh-nus"—not "Yer-AY-nus"--which just ruined all the fun.)

People—even my friends--used to see Mom out and about and ask if she could "read" them. She would spend hours on each chart, but never charge anybody, as it was "just for fun." If I was facing a crossroads in life, I'd sit down on the bed or floor in her room, and she'd say, "Let's see..." and start flipping pages in her books. She knew my chart by heart, so if she consulted the stars on a situation or new boyfriend, she'd often compare them to me in her head and mumble to herself as I waited impatiently. "What? What?" I'd ask. "Is it good, or not?" It would take her forever to give me an answer, something like: "Well, maybe, he has water in this house, fire in that house, but Taurus is very stubborn, that might be a problem..." Huh? I think Mom's method was about 20% theoretical and 80% based on knowing the person she was reading and feeling

Perplexed Planetary Pupil

the vibes they were emitting. This was easier if the person was in front of her, more difficult on the phone.

I didn't know any other kids whose mothers were astrologers. I heard about the Magi at Christmas who followed the North Star to Jesus--they were astrologers, so I figured it must be OK. Why would God give us road maps in the sky if we weren't supposed to use them to find our way? It seemed to me that the better we knew ourselves, through our charts, the better prepared we would be to improve on our weaknesses and capitalize on our strengths in life. We could be more compassionate toward others if we knew they were dealing with adverse planetary placements and stay away from the temptations to which our stars might lead us. But I could see that astrology might end up as a crutch to those trying to be good Catholics but looking for loopholes. "Father, forgive me, for I have sinned," one might confess to a priest. "Last week I was late for Mass and yelled at my kids, but, you know, Mercury was retrograde and that affects communication and travel, so... maybe go easy on me?"

In 2017, I was thrilled to stumble across a wealth of astrology information online. Finally, I could do my own chart without poring through dusty magazines and squinting at tiny charts. I could read articles online, clip paragraphs to my digital notebooks, click on links in natal charts, and draw my own conclusions. There are fun videos to watch on YouTube, like the one for The 5th Dimension's "Aquarius/Let the Sunshine In"[26] from the original 1968 Broadway musical *Hair*[27] that transported me back to an afternoon total solar eclipse in childhood spent happily doing a jigsaw puzzle in the den until it was safe to look out the window at the top of the stairs.

I signed up for webinars and joined groups of professional and amateur astrologers, seizing opportunities to learn things I'd never heard about astrology. True to my Aquarius moon, I made spreadsheets of transits, planned my life in a fun, casual way and didn't take any of it too seriously. I learned how to use astrology as a tool--like a computer--to enhance my life and become a better person, on my terms. I've tried to interest my mom in cyber-astrology, but she is sticking to her old methods. Perhaps now it's my turn to teach *her* a few things.

15

Hair Apparent

I consider my hair to be one of my superpowers, in that it is like an antenna that projects energy off the top of my head into the world and also absorbs energy into my body. It's naturally medium brown with auburn highlights. My hair has its own stories and adventures, bad days and good days, just like I do, and we feed off each other's auras. I remember how my hair looked on every important day of my life: kindergarten photo (bangs straight across, flipped on the ends); high school senior photo (parted in the middle, long and wavy); senior prom (slicked back into a neat bun); meeting my husband (in a long braid); my wedding day (curly wisps in the front, loose bun) as well as many ordinary days in between.

Hair Apparent

When I look at old photos, I notice my hair before my clothing.

I think other women in my generation understand the 'hair thing,' because we've all been there. We are the ones standing at the mirrors at the gym in the morning before work inhaling a cloud of our friend's hair spray. (I got referred to my best hair stylist ever by one such friend. I still have the stylist, the friendship maintained via biannual LinkedIn messages.)

I read or saw in a comic that Generation X has the distinct advantage of looking better than other generations as we age, because of the extreme fashions in style during our formative years. The same goes for hair as for clothing. The "go-go" 1980s called for big, big hair, and one look at my college yearbook confirms that I did, indeed, conform to that trend. My hair was big, naturally curly, and geometric. It was coiffed into a perfect triangle, poodle-style, with curly ears reaching to the synthetically enhanced shoulders of my hot pink shirt dress. And my eyebrows were launching off my face like hairy rockets.

Women from other generations look at my TBT (Throwback Thursday) Facebook posts and write, "Lol! Look at the '80s hairdo!"—for a photo I posted from 1996. It seems to me that the Boomers' long, wild hair of the

1960s and 1970s was a social statement, as are the Millennials' "Instagrammable" styles. In between them, we are the rebels who look like we stuck our fingers in the wall socket. We have a permanent (pardon the pun) look of surprise, and our hair mirrors that look: like, "What the heck is going on in the world? Really?!" In our favor, we didn't have social media then to broadcast our "bad hair day" photos. (We post them now, for comic relief.)

One year in late September, just as the Sun was entering Libra--an air sign promoting balance and harmony--a friend shared a photo on Facebook[28] of a "hair-em"--14 smiling girls dressed in a rainbow of mid-1980s pastel fashions, humongous hoop earrings, and poufy, teased hair in a variety of shapes and blonde, brown, and blondish-brown tones. The caption read: "Share this if you know someone who used too much Aqua Net in the '80's'." Everyone was smiling—of course they were! They were high on life—and hair spray fumes!

My friend thought she knew some of those girls, and 17 of her female Facebook friends (among them a Diane, Angela, Amy, Christine, Nicole, Deb, Karen, Cyndi, Monica, and Ann) gave a thumbs-up, heart, or laughing emoji of agreement. Some identified the girl ("second row, second from right") who they most closely resembled at that time. I was encouraged to see how one photo of silly hair styles could unite and uplift so many of our peers in an age when we're so preoccupied with our daily worries, responsibilities, and perceived differences of opinion. Imagine how much could be accomplished if we got together to share our stories, laughs, hopes, and dreams!

As I looked at the photo, I reflected on "the look" of the times—and a Prince tune, "U Got the Look"

(1987)[29] popped into my head, as it so often does when I think of this decade.

In the video, Sheena Easton enters a bar in Paris where Prince—in his daydream—is performing. He is "takin' aback" by this "pretty" and "tough" lady in her peach blouse, tight, black pant suit, and plume of red, curly hair.

I remembered a photo my then-boyfriend took of me in May 1987 after my college graduation. I stood on a rock in Point Judith, Rhode Island, near a restaurant where tourists ate clam cakes and chowder while watching the Block Island ferries come and go. I am smiling impishly, the ocean breeze whipping my big hair, and I'm wearing light pink cropped pants and a puffy pastel jacket, collar up, and pink flats. In the background is my brand new, sky-blue 1987 Toyota™ Celica, a gift from my parents. How could I possibly want any more from life than I had at that moment in time? By outward appearances I could not, but those innocent days were coming to an end, and I was just starting to think about what lay ahead—a new job, graduate school, more substantial relationships—and whether or not I wanted what was coming *to* me, and *at* me. But not so fast! At that moment, as Don Henley sang: "All she wants to do is dance… "[30]

Hair Apparent

16

Great (Mrs.) Scott![31]

I learned in Catechism (CCD) as a kid that you were supposed to help people out, because you never knew if they were angels testing you, or maybe actually Jesus, even though they didn't look like Him, and when you helped them you were actually showing you loved Him indirectly. I hoped He was paying attention, because I was always on the lookout for someone to help when I was growing up, and I had no shortage of those.

The problem was, as a kid I didn't really have a say over many things yet, so I had to appeal to my parents' sense of generosity and goodwill, and they weren't always so pleased with my timing. They usually went along eventually, but they didn't really say, "Now, go out and help some people today."

Great (Mrs.) Scott!

They usually just said, "Go outside for a while," probably so I would stop pestering them and let them get on with the lawn mowing or cleaning the house. So, I would walk around the block with my eyes and ears open after school, on weekends, or summer days, and I got to know some people.

Around the block, up on a hill, was a house kind of like ours, where a red-haired lady named Mrs. Scott lived by herself, I think, with her big dog Scout, who was a golden retriever. I liked Mrs. Scott because she was always happy to see me and let me pet Scout and take him for walks.

I never had a dog, just a bird—but that's a whole other story. Scout liked to go for long walks, and he smelled like a dog. Sometimes I hugged him, and he licked my face. Mrs. Scott couldn't get around as well as she used to, so she really appreciated having me walk him now and then. A couple of times I brought Scout back and it was around lunch time, but Mrs. Scott was just sitting in her kitchen by herself, not making anything, and it was dark and cold. So I said, "Hey, why don't you come on over to our house for a bite?" Then I thought when we were walking over, "I hope it's OK with Mom."

We got to my house and I went in and said, "Hi Mom, guess who I brought over for lunch?" and Mom kind of looked surprised, but she was OK after that, and Mrs. Scott came in for a grilled cheese sandwich and soup, or whatever Mom could rustle up that day. Scout would plunk himself down next to Mrs. Scott and wait for some crumbs to fall his way. Usually, I would get a look from Mom like "Really? You did this again?" but she got over it. Besides, I knew that we had plenty of food--unless it was grocery shopping day--and even extras, like the good kind of potato chips, and some nice cookies for dessert, the kind that came in the little white bag that the old guy on TV advertised, "Pepp'ridge Fahm[32] remembahs," like he was from Maine (even though the company was actually in Connecticut, and we don't talk like that). Sometimes, we dipped those big, flower-shaped molasses cookies with sugar on top[33] in our milk or tea.

It was a little extra trouble to have someone over, like setting another place and making an extra sandwich, but I think Mrs. Scott was happy for the company and went home with a little skip in her step and a bag with some apples and cookies for a snack. That made me happy, too, and I didn't mind helping Mom clean up later because I felt a little guilty about springing a guest on her last minute. I

Great (Mrs.) Scott!

figured, maybe if Mom or I were alone in our house someday, it would be nice to have someone invite us over for lunch once in a while, to feel like we weren't invisible. Also, it would make sure that our manners wouldn't get rusty.

Years later, I would always think of Mrs. Scott when I went to visit my folks, or when I saw a big dog like Scout, and when I see Scott[34] paper towels or napkins in the supermarket--Scott had like 1,000 sheets per roll or something and was safe for your septic system. It was pretty economical if you bought a huge package of 36 rolls at the big box store. I don't think Mrs. Scott was related to the paper company, though.

We never knew her first name—we just called her Mrs. Scott. Mom says she moved down to Florida in the late 1970s and we never saw her again. But in case her family reads this, they would know that their mother, or grandmother, was a great neighbor—I'm sure Jesus already knows that.

17

Nerves of 'Steele'

From a tender age, I've always kept in step with my inner drill sergeant first thing in the morning. As soon as my eyelids were open, I'd start ticking off items on my to-do list: make bed, get dressed, have breakfast with my parents, practice the organ, brush my teeth, and go to school.

Yes, I liked the feeling of triumphing over the hardest part of the day—getting out of my cozy bed—but I knew that if I dawdled even five minutes I might be late for breakfast and miss out on fifteen minutes of blissful morning radio time, during which my father and I would predictably giggle and groan over the joke of the day, and my mother and I would jot down the word of the day and note its proper spelling and usage.

Nerves of 'Steele'

My "outside world" drill sergeant, a sixty-something, pseudo-great uncle named Robert L. Steele (reliable sources told me the "L" stood not for Elmo, Elmer, or Elmwood, but Lee) *really* called the shots, and I listened.

In 1974, I sent Bob some jokes I had written, along with a wallet-sized, semi-toothless third grade photo of myself. Shortly thereafter, a neatly printed "WTIC Radio 1080" Technicolor postcard bearing Bob's smiling face, addressed to me as "Miss" in bold green marker, arrived in my mailbox. Up in my room, I read and reread his message, scrawled in fat cursive with red marker: "You're a beautiful girl, Leslie—that's all I can say. (But those JOKES! THEY'RE WORSE THAN MINE!) Sincerely, Bob." I saved the card in my special "Private—keep out" writing folder with my awards, newspaper clippings, and wild ideas.

In high school, I joined the staff of the newspaper and literary magazine and started writing articles, essays, and stories. In 1980—fall of my sophomore year--to coincide with the publication of his book, *Bob Steele--A Man and His Humor*, I decided to call the radio station and interview Bob for a feature story. Keep in mind that back then there was no Internet, so to get information on someone famous you either had to go to the library and look through piles or microfiche (tiny images stored on rolls of film you viewed through a special machine) of old newspapers and magazines, or have notes of your own dating far back. You couldn't just sneak around online and stalk people or pay the fee to have digital services get "dirt" on someone.

Considering I had only interviewed high school students and teachers to this point, I was ecstatic over how well the interview with Bob went. There were many questions I'd always wanted to ask him, and I was thrilled that he listened and gave thoughtful—yet not *too* serious—responses. Before we hung up, he made me promise to review the piece for grammatical and spelling errors. After the story ran in the paper,[35] he had one correction, which is forever seared into my mind. "Take out the 'so' in front of 'unique.' It doesn't need it." So, I removed the extraneous adverb from the absolute modifier, and submitted the essay to the 1981 *Hartford Courant* Scholastic Writing Award competition. It won a place award in the senior division (grades 10-12), and wound up on the inside back cover of the school literary magazine--the last word, according to "The Real Steele:"

In talking with this "pilot of the airwaves," I was told to use correct grammar and punctuation in this article; if everything else failed, I should at least use the English language in the way it was meant to be used. All I can say is, "i Hope i dint desapoynt U, mistur Steal!"[36]

This story isn't over yet.

Six weeks before Christmas in 1980, Bob called Mom to say he was mailing me a copy of his book for the holidays, asking her to please put it somewhere I wouldn't "stumble across it." She slid it under the living room couch and forgot about it—until Bob called on Christmas afternoon and asked me if I had received the book.

"What book?" I asked, glancing at my opened gifts under the tree. Mom gasped, went red in the face, and fetched the book where she'd hidden it, apologizing profusely. In her defense, that was the first and only time she hid something under that couch. Usually all the gifts were wrapped and under my parents' bed by the first week in December (where I would shake them and try to guess what they were).

After school got out in June of 1981, I finally got to meet my first, most famous local celebrity. I had long since moved on to other projects, like an actor promoting a film that wrapped a year ago, but it was important to follow through. Mom and I caught the bus to Hartford and walked a block to the big gold building[37] where we briefly got stuck in the elevator on the 15th floor, then waited for what seemed like an eternity in the waiting room with the big "WTIC [38]1080 AM/96.5 FM" sign on the wall. I was so excited to be there that when he came out, I just froze for a minute and choked out "nice to meet you" while shaking his hand. I'm not good at first impressions. But then Bob led us into his office, overlooking Hartford County, and graciously accepted the *Éclat* and doodled in my book. As I left, he told me to keep writing. I think I saw a twinkle in his eye. Then, Mom and I found a sale on preppy shirts in G. Fox and walked through the stylish new Richardson building to Sage Allen, where she treated me to chicken salad sandwiches and frogurt.

Recently, I pulled Bob's book from my shelf, and out flew my signed postcard. But there was something else: on the inside cover, a yellow sticky note contained my young son's penciled review: "BoB steel is a great awther."

Nerves of 'Steele'

18

Schools of Swimming (S.O.S.)

With my Sun, Jupiter, Saturn, Neptune, and Midheaven in water signs (as well as several asteroids, or minor planets), I have always loved being in and around water—bathtubs, lakes, ponds, oceans, rainstorms, puddles, fish tanks, and of course, swimming pools.

In the early Zazoo years we had little plastic pools in the backyard for me to splash around in, but as I grew older--and sprouted scales and gills--it became clear to my earth sign parents—who had a "healthy respect" for water, using it primarily for cleaning purposes—that I needed a suitably aquatic environment where I could submerge myself and paddle to my heart's content, like the mini-Mermaid that I was destined to become.

Schools of Swimming (S.O.S.)

In the mid-1970s, we joined Shady Brooke Swim and Tennis Club, a ten-minute bike ride from my house (five minutes in Mom's "tangerine machine," an orange 1970 Datsun 510[39]), and I started taking swimming lessons. I guess I was a little slow to put my head in and swim "properly"—I didn't like the feel of water in my eyes and got one "swimmer's earache" after another—and was falling behind the other kids. Rather than cast my future Olympic swimming career to the winds of fate, my mom enrolled me in the prestigious "Guppy Aquatics of Rocky Dale" (GARD) west of the Connecticut River, where the instructors assured us that since I already had some basic skills, they'd whip me into Mark Spitz (the Michael Phelps of the 1970s) shape in a few months' time. They weren't kidding about the whipping part. I still have nightmares about this place, but at least I mastered the front crawl.

It turned out that parents were not allowed in the pool area during lessons, so to her extreme dismay Mom had to sit in the lobby or out in the car in 90 degree temperatures for two hours until I was done. At the swim club she could sit on her webbed lawn chair in the shade with the other moms and watch the lessons. But she made the sacrifice so that we could go on family vacations to Cape Cod or Rhode Island and they wouldn't have to worry about getting wet and rescuing me—they could just let me venture into the depths and simply alert the nearest lifeguard should I run into any riptides or sharks. Also, because they couldn't or didn't want to swim well (my mom almost drowned swimming in a lake as a child), they approached my swimming instruction with the same zeal as they monitored my dental hygiene habits—to ensure I wouldn't fall prey to the fillings, bridges, root canals and other dental decrepitude they endured in adulthood.

One week, class ended and I was still in there long after the other kids had left. The instructor was waiting for me to dive in headfirst in the deep end from the diving board. I was resisting. I stood on that board, head down, hands together in front of me, goosebumps on my shaky legs. It was a Jekyll-and-Hyde[40] moment: I don't like to be told what to do, so I switched from Zazoo, who likes to have fun and do her own thing, to Scorpio Sun Leslie, who would stand on that board forever without caving.

Finally, as the summer sun inched lower in the sky and the evening swimmers started bunching up at the door, the guy snuck up on me, jumped once on the board, and in I went—like a penguin, not a swan. I would encounter similar gracelessness in my teen years, as I practiced for

Nerves of 'Steele'

hours to do a cartwheel and catch a baton (not at the same time). Perhaps I associated being upside down with the time Dad had to hold me by the ankles to dislodge a chive that had stuck in my throat. In any case, when I surfaced and swam toward the door, I sensed my mother was more upset than I was, even though I'd passed the final exam.

These swimming lessons paid dividends years later, as I enjoyed pool parties and lakeside vacations, as well as completed charity triathlons with friends and supervised my sons' water adventures. But I still think my parents could have saved a lot of money, time, and pain by getting me a cheap pair of goggles and some earplugs and letting me muddle about with the Shady Brooke kids.

19

I Love It in the Yoga Zone...
Wherever I Lay My Mat is My Om

(The title of this story was respectfully inspired by the early 1970s hit "Papa Was a Rollin' Stone," by the Temptations)[41]

My mother was way ahead of her time, or maybe she was influenced by the Beatles in the late 1960s--particularly George Harrison--during their transcendental meditation and Eastern philosophy phase when they traveled to India. Either way, around 1970--in her early thirties--she got into yoga as a lifestyle long before there were a million apps for it on your smartphone and a studio on every corner. She first took lessons from a local teacher, who I imagined to have a braid of hair swinging past her rear end like a metronome and a purple leotard with a secret symbol on the chest, like Lilias Folan,[42] the "Julia Child of Yoga," whose show I'd seen on public television.

I Love It in the Yoga Zone...

I thought Lilias seemed very peaceful, but if you slacked off and let your thighs touch the ground during upward facing dog, I bet she'd make you do ten chaturanga[43] pushups as punishment.

Mom might have become an instructor herself, except her hair was too short. After a while, she got tired of the hassle and just wanted to do yoga at home her own way, which is how I learned. Whenever I got stiff from sitting at my desk writing or reading for too long, I'd fold into downward dog on my orange carpet and stretch out my backside, letting my head hang down and walking in place. Every morning, I'd roll out of bed and flow into a sun salutation without thinking, reaching up to the sky and swan diving down, feeling a rush of joy at being alive and breathing fresh air into my lungs. When my nose was clogged, I'd exhale through alternate nostrils until equilibrium was restored. I could spend an hour on the floor with my legs twisted into a pretzel shape, and balance on one leg like a crane.

My precise balance helped my athletic performance, too—to Dad's consternation, I could hop on my pogo stick for ten minutes without stopping, gouging circular rings on the freshly paved driveway. And I could ride my purple bicycle with the banana seat—with yellow bananas printed on it—with my feet on the handlebars (and no helmet). If I needed some space, I'd hide behind a chair in the living room or between my bed and the wall, curled into child's pose with my head down, chest on my knees and hands wrapped around my feet. Yoga for me was like hitting the "refresh" button on a web page—it caught me up to the present moment if things became stuck or lacked clarity.

I fell away from yoga during the 1980s, distracted by college, work, and social opportunities. To stay fit, I bounced my way through aerobics classes, pumped iron, and exhausted myself on long weekend runs and cycling excursions. Though I distanced myself from "my mother's exercise," occasionally I caught myself flowing through some favorite poses while stretching or upon rising.

When my husband and I built a house in 1997, I started going to weekly classes at a yoga studio in town owned by a cute little couple in their 60s, "Carlie" and "Tom."

I was in my early thirties—as Mom had been when she started—the time of life when Saturn completes its first orbit,[44] and found myself returning to the mat to ease a career transition from systems consulting to journalism. Yoga was an essential outlet for me during the ensuing 10 years when my boys were young and I needed to get out of the house. Actually, I started freelance writing for the local newspaper to pay for Zen, and beauty. I may have been "at home" and a mommy, but I sure as heck wasn't going to give up my salon haircuts and chakra balancing.

Though I purchased the class card every other month and had the freedom to show up when my schedule permitted, I typically arrived fifteen minutes early to claim my favorite mat--third from left in the front row—and do some spinal rocking and breathing, lulled by the sound of flutes, sitars, and soft chanting. Heaven help anyone who got there first and took my mat. I couldn't even concentrate on the class, preoccupied as I was casting dagger looks at the unsuspecting innocent in "my spot." I had to overcome a powerful urge to go up to them, take all their stuff, throw it on the mat behind, and scream, "No one takes my mat!" But I was too nice, and ended up getting all hot and sweaty, even if it wasn't a heated class, my toes and teeth clenched tightly. Most of the time, though, I got my mat, and would leave glowing and mellow, as if floating on a cloud, and be extra nice to everyone for the rest of the day.

Years later, when Tom and Carlie closed up shop to teach senior yoga at the community center, I took a couple of heated power classes at a new yoga place down the road that used to be a chicken restaurant. But I hated it, because I couldn't get the chicken smell out of my nostrils and was distracted by twentysomething girls taking selfies of themselves in various poses and older ladies' constant chattering. I really preferred the normal classes where you could flop down in Savasana (corpse pose) at the end with a blanket over you, not in a puddle of your own sweat.

On a sunny but bitingly cold winter day in February, I visited a studio in a neighboring town that held potential to be my new yoga home. The owner asked me if I was certified to teach classes. I smiled, thanked her and drove home, where I rolled out my mat and did a few quick poses before settling down to work at my desk.

Online sources[45] attribute the phrase "Wherever you go, there you are" to Confucius, and it speaks to my search for the perfect yoga site.

Today, my mat lies alongside the treadmill in a slim space I've claimed between the pantry shelves, foosball table, and an old stereo in the basement gym. I prop up my tablet and move through my poses with yoga masters streaming from beautiful locales around the world—pristine lakes, green forests, wild prairies, and lofty mountain

I Love It in the Yoga Zone…

perches. When I'm done, I click "Like," close the tablet, and lie on my dry mat for five minutes, sighing as I soak up the bliss.

    Finally, I'm home.

20

The Stride Hyper of Smellingdung

(An adventure in the spirit of the legend of the Pied Piper of Hamelin[46])

Our story begins in the picturesque village of Smellingdung, where when the wind blows just right you are accosted by the scent of cows at work. The wise mayor, sensing a need for a place for children to learn to swim, their elders to play pickleball and do water aerobics, and women to shake maracas and dance wildly in large groups to Latin American pop music, built a grand gymnasium with glass facades on several acres of woodland near a busy roundabout. At dawn, when the sun rose in the east and painted the sky in stripes of orange, red, and pink, it blinded those slaving away in the wellness center, so they couldn't watch the morning news or sports on their tiny televisions while they ellipticized.

But there were plenty of parking spots for everyone's crossovers, pickups, minivans, and even a gas company truck. The mayor visited the Family Aquatics and Recreation Megacenter (FARM) and saw that it was good, indeed.

Soon after the grand opening, a group of gym rats began to congregate at the FARM at 5 a.m. during the week, before the roosters crowed and work and family responsibilities clamored for their attention.

The rats complained loudly to management that they wanted to get rid of the fat and step up their game. So management hired Sam (short for Samantha), a fitness enthusiast often seen striding along the streets of the village clad in multicolored spandex clothing and running sneakers, to train the rats. Sam sweated the fat out of them—into great puddles on the floor--through multiple reps of pushups, burpees, jumping jacks, and sprints, accompanied by the greatest pop hits of the 1980s and '90s. The rats had so much fun with Sam that they barely realized they were working hard. Some of them started competing in crazy mud runs, charity triathlons, and half marathons, having *Rocky*[47] moments and high-fiving each other (though this, unfortunately, caused one rat's shoulder to dislocate temporarily). Sam became known as the Stride

Hyper because of her contagious enthusiasm for running long distances at a steady pace.

Encouraged by the rats' progress, Sam started to "push the envelope" by doing things no one had dared do before, like holding outdoor boot camp classes, setting up a contraption on which the rats could hang from straps to build muscle,[48] and working out along with the rats. She showed them how to eat "clean" and told them where to buy protein powder. The rats were drawn to Sam like moths to a flame.

Despite her astounding success with the rats, Sam itched to return to her home in the sunny south to train new rats by the ocean. Before she left, the rats got together and threw Sam a big sendoff party, complete with grilled chicken on a stick, little shrimp cups, and a chocolate dipping fountain for dessert. One of the rats, a professional chef, graciously hosted the gang at his house. As the summer sun set, the rats gathered around the fire pit and gave Sam some beautiful gifts to thank her for her service and her friendship. They didn't want her to go, but wished her the best with her new company, RatRoadRacer.

After Sam's departure, the rats went back to the FARM but quickly drifted apart without her guidance. One by one (and two by two) the rats departed for other gyms where they could exercise for half the cost. The triathletes were disheartened but stayed on the FARM to use the heated Olympic-sized pool. Some just didn't care, having stayed too long in the sauna.

Never one to throw in the towel, I stuck around, doing my own thing. One morning I opened my eyes after stretching and meditating (my black tights dotted with purple rubber bits from a gym-issued yoga mat) to find a grizzled man leaning over me, looking confused. His tee shirt read: 'I may be old, but I got to see all the cool bands.' "It's about time," he said. "I thought you fell asleep." It *was* time—for me to work out at home and write the story of the day the Stride Hyper freed the rats from the FARM, and all the little stories that sprang from that serendipitous event.

21

(Not So) Hot to Trot

On the Sunday afternoon before Thanksgiving, I was standing in the 12-items-and-fewer line at the grocery store, waiting to pay for a few things I couldn't get from the Bus o' Sprouts that came every Saturday morning: ground pork to make Memere's special stuffing; a bag of frozen turnips for my special whipped turnip "Mrs." Puff,[49] named after SpongeBob's blowfish driving teacher; a bottle of "sensitive skin" pomegranate body wash; two tins of sugar-free mints; and a bottle of teen boys' "yummy gummy" daily vitamins.

While scanning, the cashier asked what excitement I had planned for the week. Normally, I patronize the self-checkout to avoid this sort of inquiry, but the scent of cinnamon and holiday carols had me feeling somewhat civil.

(Not So) Hot to Trot

"I'm running in the Road Race on Thursday," I said, leaving out "Manchester" because everyone in Northeast-central Connecticut region knows someone also running, walking, or cheering from the sidelines at this event—like the woman behind me in line, it turned out, whose sister was planning to run as well. "Good for you!" chirped the cashier, fascinated to learn I had been running for years, yet only on MRR number four. "Are you running with anyone, or just by yourself?" I put my breath mints in my tote and picked up my bags. "Oh, um, I'll probably meet up with someone there," I stammered, desperate to be on my way. "Well, have fun," she called after me, greeting the next customer with equal exuberance.

As happens so often in life, an everyday exchange can set you back on your heels, just when you thought everything was proceeding according to plan. Of course I'd been training for the Race for months, running five to seven miles every weekend.

I alternated weeks on the rails-to-trails wooded path (my happy place) and on local hilly country roads as the leaves burst into a fiery kaleidoscope of color, got whipped around on a rainy night, then slept under an early blanket of wet, heavy snow before I even noticed that the mums I so lovingly cared for in October had shriveled and the pumpkins, once wickedly grinning ghouls, were now mushy-mouthed gourds begging to be pitched into the woods by a 15 year-old aiming for the farthest tree.

I would be happy finishing the almost-five-mile loop in 50 minutes, but unlike the Hartford Marathon, a "serious" event, very few ran this turkey trot to set any records. There were a few dozen elite racers clad in shorts, gloves, and tank tops jumping up and down in 35-degree weather in the under-30-minute corrals, eager to make their mark and hop back in their sweatpants to nurse a hot chocolate before the remaining 90 percent of the crowd made it around the corner of Main Street. These were the ones people watching from their cozy living rooms could see flying toward the finish line, Americans striding along with Kenyans, Australians, British, and Mexicans—many fresh from the Olympics.

The slight discomfort I experience from rising early and running in the unpredictable New England autumn weather makes me grateful that I *can* run, in the first place, and that I get to go home, shower, and enjoy a delicious turkey dinner with loved ones later that day. Passing St. James Catholic Church in the final mile gives me the opportunity to say a quick prayer before I "dig deep" and

(Not So) Hot to Trot

sprint for the finish line, waving at the cameras as I do my little victory dance. For a brief moment, I am a champion, having conquered my lesser self. I've earned that glass of wine, seconds of green bean casserole, a slice of pumpkin *and* chocolate cream pie.

But I think the magic of the Race lies in the connections people make—and renew—from year to year. It is the "six degrees of Safety Man[50] (a gregarious orange flight suit-clad Road Race legend)" factor--you are bound to bump into (often literally) someone you know at this event. While standing in my usual spot just behind the 42-minute seeded, or qualified, runners, I have reunited with cousins, co-workers, and high school friends—pretty serendipitous, if you glance downhill at the sea of 12-to-15,000 participants and spectators flooding the main and side streets of central "Silk City."[51] My former boss-- now retired from state service--ambles (as "running is such a strong word") and networks along the route, finishing with nearly 50 handshakes.

Most years, I usually get stuck climbing the long hill at the beginning behind a family in medieval armor with two people in a horse costume, a "Whac-a-mole"[52] game, an entire Thanksgiving dinner, and people stopping by the side of the road to accept cans of beer or a swig of liquor from merry bystanders. Simultaneously, I am chased by five hundred Santas with bells, along with a few strips of bacon, the Incredibles, Gumby, and a Rubik's Cube. And these are the "serious" runners.

In my nightmares—dreams where I am failing high school despite having earned my master's degree--I am that person who finishes the Race last--after they've rolled up the finish line and TV cameras and everyone's hopped back on the shuttle bus, gone home to eat turkey, watch the Macy's parade and Westminster Dog Show with the kids, toss a football in the backyard. The saving grace, the world of difference between annoyance and glee, between failure and a treasured memory, is running the Race with good friends.

I had never been to the Race growing up, as my parents were always cooking dinner on Thanksgiving morning. In any case, they made every effort to avoid a) sporting events, b) extreme weather, and c) any combination of a) and b). Extreme weather for them included temperatures lower than 50 and higher than 70 degrees, regardless of wind, and any precipitation heavier than random raindrops. Until I met Millee and Carine, my running buddies, I didn't know anyone in my age group game for such an adventure.

The November I turned 50, I ran my first Road Race dressed as Yoda from Star Wars, with a neon green jacket over black patterned tights and a goofy olive-green hat with ears and "winged" socks to match. I could have been Princess Leia, but my white tights showed the dog hair and the cinnamon rolls kept sliding off my ears. Millee, the artist, forged a Chewbacca costume out of fake fur and foil.

Carine, a French-American triathlete, accountant and mom of two, wore her Wonder Woman costume and waved her seeded status to keep us company. Usually we appeared to be standing still as she flew by in pursuit of a first place in her age category.

Before the race, we met a big-hearted, red-bearded giant in a ski cap--an old classmate of Millee's--who looked like he should have been mushing his dogs like Yukon Cornelius from *Rudolph the Red nosed Reindeer*. We felt like he was looking out for our little misfit group, protecting us from the Abominable Snow Monster.

Someone took our picture right before the National Anthem filled us with pride and giddy anticipation, along with a soul-warming shot of adrenaline. After the gun went off, we stuck together until my shoe slipped off my fluttery foot mid-hill and a kind woman held the crowd back so I could hobble over and retrieve it. My friends waited as I caught up, worried I'd been trampled. We crossed the finish line seconds apart--arms raised in triumph--and high-fived each other.

The "Force" was with us that day.

The following year, Carine and I ran the Race together dressed as runners trying to stay dry and warm (she wore her Wonder Woman compression socks over her tights). I wore thick compression socks, not caring to repeat my slippery-Yoda-sock stunt. Before the race, some friends from our running club met us at the veterans' hall and took our photo for Facebook. We tagged our friend "Chewie," who was in our thoughts and prayers that year, her absence felt in our increasingly serious discussions and shorter jaunts.

Last year I went through the motions—bus, line up, run, bus, home, dinner—with a heavy heart despite the crisp, sunny day. While I waited on my designated manhole cover for the race to begin, the man standing to my left, cheerful in his yellow hooded sweatshirt, began to ask me for advice on starting a running program.

Despite my recent decline in enthusiasm for the sport—akin to the bearded, haggard Forrest Gump abruptly coming to a halt in the middle of Utah, en route to Monument Valley[53]--I summoned enough of a spark to encourage him, feeling more hopeful than I had in months as we lost each other in the mob of merrymakers.

As Thanksgiving 2018 drew closer, and well-meaning friends and forecasters warned runners to stay inside lest they freeze their drumsticks and giblets at the annual turkey trot, Zazoo nagged at me to carry through with the only race I would run all year. "You wimp!" she scolded. "Put on your face mask and stop whining!"

Carine posted a photo of herself and a friend, only the sparkle in their eyes visible amidst multiple hats and neck gaiters. Though she told me not to "beat myself up" and "there will be other races," I felt a pang of regret watching videos of waddling participants bundled up like Ralphie's younger brother Randy in *A Christmas Story*, unable to lift their arms. While the voice of reason reminded me that over 4,000 people of 12,000 also opted out of the race, I insisted on running five miles on the treadmill before I wore the purple race shirt—only "rookies" tempted fate like that.

Leslie B. Placzek / Adventures of Zazoo Plazz

22

Miss Merry Moonwalk

A few years ago, I started binge-watching a reality TV show called *Dance Moms*[54] that had premiered on a channel that should provide its (primarily) female audience with a 'lifetime' supply of tissues for all the tears its dramatic programming induced. From her studio in Pittsburgh, PA, with occasional jaunts to dance competitions in exciting places like Los Angeles and Miami, dance instructor Abby Lee Miller put a small group of girls through the rigorous training required to succeed in the cutthroat world of dance and show business. The show was a guilty pleasure for me--I always felt like I needed to take a shower afterward—because it featured a bunch of glammed-up moms confined to an enclosed viewing area above the dance floor, going at each other like hamsters in a cage.

Miss Merry Moonwalk

Every few episodes, one of the moms would have to leave the group, usually for asserting that her daughter was the most talented—because her picture was on top of the pyramid that week—or for sinking her perfectly manicured claws into Abby for dressing the nine-year-olds like little strippers. On her way out the door, the exiled mom would usually protest, as her mascara ran down her face, that she hadn't come to make friends, but to give her daughter, the future star, the very best training. Like rogue hamsters, the dance mom bullies weren't necessarily bad—they just behaved poorly because they felt insecure and threatened. Post-exile, everyone would go back to running peacefully on their exercise wheels or sewing their costumes—until the next episode.

When I got hooked on the show, my oldest son had just earned his Junior Black Belt from a local karate studio. My minivan looked like the storeroom at the mall's sporting goods store and smelled worse than the Red Sox' locker room after the 2004 World Series, when they trampled the "Curse of the Bambino."[55]

Our living room had transformed into a year-round Boy Scout campsite, and it seemed that I was always putting down toilet seats. I was thankful not to have to spend hours shopping, sewing, and dressing my children for dance competitions, complete with glamourous makeup and hairstyles.

Yet Zazoo held tight to my own dancing adventures from 40 years ago, buried in my memories like a pair of outgrown tap shoes shoved to the bottom of a garment bag in my parents' basement with a couple of mothballs and Granny's afghan for company.

Unearthing my own dancing adventures made me feel sorry for the girls on the show, who just wanted to dance and have fun, and for Abby Lee, whose job it was to get these little caterpillars to do their best, concentrate on the routines, and emerge from their cocoons months later as brilliant butterflies, fluttering in formation across the stage. Perhaps someday one of those girls will decide—as did Abby Lee—that she would rather teach others to dance than perform, and she will credit Abby Lee with inspiring her to do so.

Back in the early 1970s, when "reality TV" consisted of Allen Funt saying, "Smile—you're on *Candid Camera*"[56] to unsuspecting pedestrians on the street, and Abby Lee was taking her first shuffle ball changes in her mother's dance studio, my mother and her sister, Olivienne, brought me and my cousin Katy to the basement of a local

Miss Merry Moonwalk

Episcopal church to learn dance from Miss Meredith "Merry" Moonwalk. I imagine Mom was looking for an outlet for my considerable five-year-old energy, and a way for me to grow closer to my cousin, who was ten months older, though in my grade.

I was a sturdy kid whose chubby legs were better suited to rigorous stomping than pirouetting on my toes in a tutu. To this day, I can't get my leg to stay on a barre. But I had a fire in me, such that once I started tapping I couldn't stop. Dad made me a special strip of polished wood to dance on in the kitchen so I wouldn't mark up the vinyl floor. I used to get so excited when the music started that I would lose myself in the moment, hoofing with exuberance unmatched by any other activity.

Once when I was around six, in the finale of a tapping frenzy, I tapped all the way off the board into the cage of my canary, Tweety, knocking it off its stand onto the dining room floor in a flurry of feathers and seeds. It was at that moment my parents realized that Tweety—a bit ruffled but strangely smug on his little perch--was the reincarnated bird my father had accidentally sent to its demise in the 1940s by opening a second-story balcony door into its cage. I had inherited the canary-cage-collision gene.

When I met her, Miss Merry was about 37, with short black hair. She was very close to her mother, a feisty lady who kept the books and had taught *her* to dance as a child, as well as how to run a dance business, which came in handy when she opened her first studio at age 16.

Thankfully, she didn't put up our pictures in a pyramid every week so you could see where you stood. "Too bad, Leslie, you got bumped down to level two this week—remember, your timing was off." But she did waddle around the room like a duck to mirror our less-graceful moves. And the *whole class* had to repeat the routine when any one of us messed up, with no exceptions. We did it over and over until it was as close to perfect as could be expected, though we ached to get on with it, already, and start something new.

Miss Merry thickened my skin for taking organ lessons at age seven and ignited in me a love for all types of dancing. My style falls somewhere between SpongeBob's neighbor Squidward's free-form float and Seinfeld character Elaine's jerky-turkey hand jive. She also gave me the confidence which comes from performing onstage in front of an audience, albeit a "warm" audience of attentive mothers, fidgety siblings, loyal friends, and softly snoring fathers.

Miss Merry Moonwalk

At my first recital, decked out as a "dancing poodle" in a sky-blue leotard over white tights with little hairy snowballs stuck to my abdomen, rear, and ears, I step ball changed to the front row, relishing my moment under the lights and the glint of a camera flash. Suddenly I turned, and seeing Katy in the back row, proceeded to grab her hand and tow her to the front, to the horror of my mother and aunt and the delight of Bunny, who said she had never seen anything so cute in her whole life. Memere smiled.

The 1972 costume was a jazzy red, white, and blue sequin number with fringe over black tights and a little firecracker crown—my favorite, sewn by Mom (and Dad) with a passion I suspect surpassed that of Betsy Ross for her flag. Rumor has it that after a near-riot erupted one year over which shade of green to buy for the "Crocodile Rock" outfits, Miss Merry's mother advised her to wrest the reins of costume decision-making from students and parents.

My dancing career ended in 1973, after an extremely feverish, spotty case of chicken pox miraculously cleared up in time for my final recital. But Miss Merry kept teaching for decades, training stars for Broadway and leaving the studio in the hands of her great-grand-niece, who may one day teach my granddaughter—or grandson. As Sonny and Cher sang (as my toe taps along): "The Beat Goes On..."[57]

23

Focus on Your Calling

One morning in early December, at the end of a week when I had been particularly efficient and run out of legitimate ways to procrastinate on writing this book, I stumbled across one of those online quizzes you take in right-brain mode, before your inner lawyer can advise you otherwise—"no, don't press that--aaaugh! Floating down my caffeinated river of hope in my inner tube of inflated expectations, I was frustrated when, after providing my 'fun' e-mail address and land line number, I did not, in fact, receive a $1,000 gift card with which to purchase my holiday gifts in cyber-Santa land. However, I did receive many phone calls, an hour or two later when I was in my office, blessed inspiration miraculously coursing through my veins and out my fingertips to the screen.

Focus on Your Calling

While I consider the telephone a useful tool for communicating in emergencies and for maintaining relationships, I think one cordless set upstairs and one in the kitchen is adequate, given our attachment to our cell phones.

My husband, perhaps in competition with the Jerry Lewis MDA telethon (retroactively) or trying to conserve his energy, installed two phones upstairs, one in the kitchen, and two in the basement, including one corded dinosaur at his desk. To make my work-at-home life even more pleasant (and ensure I think of him during the day while he is at the office), he set the ringtone (at max volume) to the sound of a Dalek[58] from *Dr. Who* running over a player piano pumping out Scott Joplin's "The Entertainer"—on a two-minute loop. After the fourth round, I yanked the guts out of each phone, threw them across the room, and spent the rest of the afternoon in heavenly silence except for the dog barking at a delivery truck.

When he got home, my husband repaired the phones and gave me a secret password to type in to take the phone offline during the day, sending robocalls to voicemail. The problem was that once I took the phone out of commission, I forgot to turn it back on, and I never checked voicemail, so content was I in my little bubble of productivity. Obsessive message checking—and saving, sometimes for years—was Gray's job, along with tinkering with and hoarding obsolete electronic gadgets that "might be useful" in the event of a *Mars Attacks*-style alien invasion (where he would save the planet by rigging a device that broadcasts the theme song from *Laverne and Shirley*[59] into their spaceship at high volume, bursting their bulbous brains).

Listening to the Vince Guaraldi Trio's *A Charlie Brown Christmas* makes me want to curl up on the couch with the dog (if she'd let me) and a glass of pumpkin flax milk egg nog with nutmeg and watch the *Peanuts* gang dance and Snoopy decorate his doghouse for at least the 53rd time (since it premiered on December 9, 1965). Inevitably I would hop along with them, playing the air piano and swiveling from side to side like Frieda, the "naturally curly-haired"[60] girl in the purple dress and saddle shoes. That show brought me back to the first phone I remember—the gold, wall-mounted rotary dial one in my parents' kitchen, where you had no choice but to sit on the collapsible yellow stool to talk, as the cord was only as long as your arm. Mom was thrilled to get a longer cord, so she could talk while she cooked dinner—a freedom akin to putting the dog on a 100-foot run staked in the backyard when she's been confined to a 6-foot-long nylon rope all her life.

Early on, I gravitated toward that golden phone like glitter from Christmas cards stuck to your hands, or socks from the dryer clinging to your legs. Mom would be deep into a conversation, look down, and I was in the hallway, back to the closet, or face down with my chin resting on my hands, grasping at snippets of truth as if I were catching pearl bath oil beads from heaven. I begged to call people—grandparents, aunts, uncles, friends—to share news of a good report card, invite them over, or just to say 'hello' and let them know I was thinking of them. There were so few phones and minutes in the day, and so many people to call! Now, we have more phones than people in our house, and spend our time searching for ways to stop the phone from ringing rather than talking to the loved ones who remain.

Later on that December day, in a gesture of hope and goodwill, I approached the silver-and-black toy soldier phone standing at his post near the microwave oven and pressed three keys, leaving myself open to a possible onslaught of time-wasting telemarketers. Ten minutes later, the phone rang. It was Aunt Georgia, my dad's sister, who lived about a mile down the road, though we hadn't seen each other in over a year. As we caught up on family news and holiday plans, I sipped my squash smoothie with nutmeg and gave thanks I had freed the phone from its prison, at least for a little while. I was Zazoo talking on the big phone again, only this time without any cord.

24

Cleaning Troubles, Oils and Grumbles

A couple of years ago for my birthday, Gray bought me an essential oil diffuser, a white plastic mushroom cap-like combination lava lamp and old-school humidifier like my parents installed in my bedroom with a dollop of Vick's menthol oil when I had a bad cold as a child and couldn't breathe.

At first I cranked it full blast in the downstairs powder room opposite my office—in the career bagua of the house--to neutralize the detrimental effects of having three males visit it on a "regular" basis.

For that purpose, it really didn't matter what kind of oil I used, as long as it smelled pleasant.

Plus, it was cheaper and more sustainable than buying those little twist-open air fresheners at the dollar store (which my son's music teacher cleverly repurposed to muffle his trumpet).

I could have stopped there, with my six-oil starter set: lemongrass, lavender, peppermint, orange (which Jack said smelled like cat pee), tea tree, and eucalyptus. But the lady in the product's video moved her diffuser around her spare, sparkling white house, her long, straight hair skimming her back as she calmly poured water and two or three shots of different oils in the reservoir, replaced the top, and settled cross-legged on her bed in her body-hugging leggings and camisole top.

Perhaps if I, too, used my diffuser more, in different rooms, I could reach a higher level of consciousness like this woman. I wondered if there were oils to make husbands load the dishwasher, wean teenagers off video games, and keep Deranged Dogs from jumping on guests and tearing through handbags.

Curiosity piqued, I began to search for essential oils online and backed out of the rabbit hole[61] three hours later, mouth open and drooling onto my keyboard after clicking on square after colorful square of tantalizing "cozy winter diffuser blends" and "magic oils for wealth and prosperity you must try *now*," ending up on a page describing how to make my own dryer sheets. The diffuser had long since beeped at me and fallen asleep, out of steam. My hands were sweaty, mouth dry, contact lenses stuck to my eyeballs.

Scent possibilities tickled my olfactory fancy: there were so many oils, so little time!

I ordered a few more basic oils—lemon, bergamot, vetiver, cedarwood, and rose—for cleaning, laundry, and skin lotions. Playing with essential oils made me feel like one of the witches in Shakespeare's *Macbeth*, huddled over their caldron, tossing in newts' eyes and frogs' toes and incanting their spells.

Then I discovered the perfect scent—a woodsy, musky,"eau de yoga class" oil called patchouli. I put a few drops in my diffuser while working in my office, and immediately felt soothed, uplifted, and warmed down to my toes. One day, after Jack said, "Mom's sniffing her hippie oil again," I realized that this scent reminded me of Lestoil™, my mother's favorite all-purpose cleaner since 1970 (and *her* mother's, since the '50s),[62] and recoiled a little.

Cleaning Troubles, Oils and Grumbles

That stuff was in every toilet in our house, and it bubbled back up after you flushed it, lodging in your nostrils for days. Mom was of the "It's not clean until all bacteria, good and bad, is dead" school of domestic hygiene. Where she couldn't use bleach or Lestoil™ she stuck moth balls, which killed everything else.

As a child, I thought they made this stuff for me, since my name was Les (lie) and cleaning is "toil," like the witches' "double, double, toil and trouble, fire burn and caldron bubble."[63] Was I destined to stand over the bowl sniffing this stuff my whole life? The concept horrified me so that I vowed when I grew up, I'd find natural cleaning alternatives to get the job done without knocking myself out—in other words, "less toil" both on my body and the earth.

These days, I clean almost exclusively with baking soda, vinegar, and essential oils. When Gray gagged at the smell of white vinegar and water on the kitchen floor, I snuck in some lavender. I guess I can tolerate strong scents, since the linings of my nose were singed with pine dynamite and I was descended from a line of pickle-palates. I can drink straight vinegar (with a beet juice chaser) without flinching.

Given that my parents' motto has always been "everything in moderation," I'm sure Mom saw the value in a powerful product that removed the grease from Dad's "working on the car and mowing the lawn" clothes, properly diluted with water. She might have seen the 1978 commercial in which a woman complains to a bottle of Lestoil™ about its strong smell. Nodding toward her husband's spotless shirts, the big-nosed bottle replies that if it "didn't smell so strong, it wouldn't work so good. To smell me is to love me!"[64]

I had no occasion to test its effectiveness until one spring Friday evening when Gray and the boys went to see a superhero movie and I stayed home, looking forward to a relaxing evening soaking my feet in an Epsom salt bath and painting my toes.

As I was fetching the mint green-and-white foot spa from the top shelf of my closet, it hooked onto the little yellow basket with my nail polishes I'd stored there, safely out of the Diva Dog's reach. In super-slow motion, as in a cheesy movie scene, I yelled "Nooooooo!" as the basket bounced off the rug, bottles ricocheting off the dresser and smashing onto the still-new strip of tan carpet—not the pink, peach, or clear polish, but the deepest scarlet—staining it immediately.

Cleaning Troubles, Oils and Grumbles

I lunged for my phone and searched "how to remove nail polish from rug," which luckily produced about 150,000 results. After hours of scrubbing with other products—polish remover, glass cleaner, vinegar, rubbing alcohol, and shaving cream—and wailing "out, damned spot" like Lady Macbeth failed to remove the unfortunate, glaring reminder of my selfish quest for relaxation and rejuvenation, I finally threw in the sponge.

As I considered the pathetic results of my most fervent efforts, I had an idea. Pouring a splash of Lestoil™ into a bucket of water, I threw open a window and hoped for the best, grunting as I swept a rag over the prickly, pink patches of formerly-fluffy fibers. I had brought in the SWAT team, to little avail—the blot remains, to this day, like a chalk silhouette at a crime scene--but the smell made me a little nostalgic—for the first five minutes. "This too will pass," it assured me. Then I muttered a few choice spells, tossed the sludge down the toilet, and cranked up the diffuser.

25

The Lollipop Ladies

For a short time between first and third grades, it seemed like every time I passed Mrs. Toffee, my favorite crossing guard (or Lollipop Lady, as they are named in Australia and the United Kingdom for the round traffic signs they carry), on my way home from school, she was patrolling by the red fence at the corner house, enjoying the sun while Sammy Davis Jr.'s mellow voice belted out "The Candy Man" [65] from her little portable radio.

I didn't have to cross the street, but sometimes I would slow down a bit so I could see her hustle the other kids to safety without missing a beat.

The Lollipop Ladies

She was as warm as Alice, the *Brady Bunch's* housekeeper, but with the energy of Billie Jean King, the fiery tennis champion and change agent.

One day, the substitute crossing guard, Mrs. Gumdrop, saw me coming and fluttered toward me like a hummingbird, chirping "Hello!" as I approached the intersection. As she held out her arms toward me, smiling like our dental hygienist before she shoved cotton balls in my mouth and painted bubble gum fluoride all over my teeth, I gagged, burst into tears, and ran all the way home.

Mom didn't understand why I had reacted so strongly against "that lovely woman whom everyone adores," even after Mrs. Gumdrop had written a note on flowery stationery apologizing for startling me and vowing to make it right between us. In any case, I had pledged my loyalty to Mrs. Toffee, placed her in the "Lollipop Lady Hall of Fame."

I could not say why I recoiled from Mrs. Gumdrop that day. Perhaps I was deep in meditation about my afternoon snack or winding down from the rigors of a day in second grade. I may have been counting my steps, two per sidewalk square—avoiding the cracks—from school to home. It is possible that I reacted with a jerk and raw emotions the way that Disturbed Dog does, by whacking me in the nose, lip, or eye when I lean over to kiss her goodnight and she startles awake.

You would think I'd learn to "let sleeping dogs lie"[66] by this time. Could it be that the subtle smells and swirls attracting—or repelling--two dogs sniffing each other's behinds also pass between humans (at higher levels), but social conventions have taught us to disregard, and override, these instincts?

I realized that, my entire life, I have been reacting to people and situations with pre-social media immediacy: she's nice—smile! He's bad—angry face. This worked well when protecting my boys from dubious influences, such as TV shows with chuckling purple dinosaurs. Instead, we watched *Sesame Street* and *Mr. Rogers' Neighborhood*--my childhood favorites--and read books. In those familiar worlds, I shared the love I had discovered as a child—for trolleys, and sneakers tossed in the air, and skinny, blue "monsters hiding at the end of books."[67]

This instinct also alerted me to some possible disappointments in the workplace. After meeting a new supervisor--in his dark blue suit and tie--and shaking his hand, I thought he was aloof and cold. When he cut me off mid-greeting, the silence I allowed to fall between us destroyed any possibility of my helping him adjust to his new job in the future. I left the following month, despite having loved every moment of the previous three years in that place spent working with a wonderful, irreplaceable team.

Mom boiled it down to astrological placements the other night, after she lectured me about taking more Vitamin D3 "now that you're over 50, dear," and collagen powder: "Put it in your coffee!"

She mumbled something about my birth chart. "Venus and Mars in Sagittarius... third house of communications... 26 degrees... near the Galactic Center." "Galactic what?" I asked. "Look it up on your computer," she said, before hanging up to get ready for bed.

The next morning, while smooshing yellow globules into a glass of hot lemon water, I clicked open a few "scientific" articles about black holes and cosmic energy boosts. I'm as confused as before—and channeling Carl Sagan for guidance--but now I understand why so many of my fun-loving, athletic, and adventurous friends have been Sagittarians, born between the last week of November and mid-December (including my Dynamite Dog, Bebe).

Though a few of those relationships combusted as suddenly as they began, they were wild rides—straight from the divine pipeline to my heart!

I recently watched a video of Sammy Davis, Jr. singing his signature hit in 1972, in which he is wearing tinted, gold-rimmed glasses, a lemon yellow shirt with wide lapels, and a snazzy plaid jacket (that is the exact pattern of my new Christmas tablecloth), with green fringe on the breast pockets. "Mister Show Business" lent his name to the Greater Hartford Open--a Connecticut PGA golf tournament--from 1973 to 1988. He often played in the Celebrity Pro-Am at Wethersfield Country Club and--after 1985--at the Tournament Players Club in Cromwell. I didn't start volunteering at the "GHO," as most locals referred to it then, until the early 1990s--with the Greater Hartford Junior Chamber of Commerce (Jaycees)--but I recall seeing "SDJ" on the news with the other big names teeing up in the Insurance Capital of the World.

It seems that Sammy Davis, Jr. initially disliked "The Candy Man" because it was too "saccharine" and almost didn't record it for the movie *Willy Wonka and the Chocolate Factory*, which would have deprived the world of his Sagittarian talent, and him of his only number-one hit in

The Lollipop Ladies

1972, subsequent Grammy Award nomination in 1973, and many other successes.

And I may never have written about tough Mrs. Toffee, now in her nineties, born on the 27th of November.

26

Three in the Afternoon

When I was a baby, Mom put me down in my crib for my afternoon nap, as usual. Around mid-afternoon, she recalls, she was changing my diaper when suddenly I projected a missile of unruly excrement so powerfully and passionately it hit the wall and bounced up toward the ceiling. Perhaps she was referring to this incident when she said, "You were a pistol."

Fortunately, the stain blended in as the walls were a pea-soupy chartreuse, as were most of my baby clothes, because no one knew in those days if they were having a girl or a boy. Pepere even bought me a little toy dump truck, certain that I--the youngest of four granddaughters--would be a boy.

Three in the Afternoon

I threw my blocks and logs in it, transporting them to various construction sites in the living room and backyard.

After Mom had grabbed a mask and cleaned me up, I sat in my crib and smiled as she strategized how to clean the walls thoroughly and make dinner before Dad came home. She must have brought in the trusty Lestoil,™ a bucket, mop, maybe a ladder to banish the uppermost remnants. After cleaning, Mom was exhausted. She always got winded around three p.m. and needed to sit down, watch her TV show, and have a snack to recharge. Perhaps this incident was enough to convince them not to have more children—one of me seemed to be on a par with raising 1970s TV family *The Waltons*. "Good night, Zazoo!" Once Dad came home at five p.m. and swapped his suit jacket for a Fred Rogers[68]-style cardigan, an ocean of calm washed over us, and all would be forgiven, if not forgotten—at least until they painted the walls.

I wonder whether I take after Mom, in that I seem to be in control of business and life in general until about three in the afternoon, when the doo-doo hits the wall, mostly figuratively—except for when the boys were babies and the dog was a puppy--and I feel like I could use a helping hand. Yet this ethereal hour drops a golden slipper of potential, like in the 1988 movie *Working Girl*, when investment banking executive Katharine (played by Sigourney Weaver) breaks her leg skiing and her assistant Tess (Melanie Griffith), with her "head for business and bod for sin"[69] sweeps into action, transforming the staid into the stellar and saving the day. It is the time of day when my inner *Cat in the Hat*[70] shows up to juggle cake, cup, and fish atop a ball while Thing 1 and Thing 2 fly kites in the hallway. Somehow the mess gets cleaned up before my husband comes home, dinner (usually) cooking and the Devoted Dog by the door, tail wagging in welcome.

I now find myself in the mid-afternoon of life, a time when stuff hits the wall, and somehow it helps to talk to, or hear about, someone who is dealing with the same sort of mess. You don't need anyone to clean it up for you, blame you for it, or tell you to lie down. No, what you need right now is a refreshing shower and a foot bath, some cold lemonade or a hot cup of tea. You need someone to say, "It's OK! At least *your* kid didn't throw up in the minivan on the way to a wedding!" You need a friend to come over for coffee and ignore the dust on the mantel and the rings on the kitchen table, someone who will send you one of those nice bouquets of little honeydew and cantaloupe

Three in the Afternoon

flowers, with chocolate-covered strawberries on sticks, that you can nibble on or offer to guests at the holidays, when your father-in-law has just passed away.

If my life were a movie, I'd have a friend like Cynthia (Joan Cusack) in *Working Girl*, who would walk with me, root for me, pretend to be my secretary when Harrison Ford stopped by, and scream at the top of her lungs when I got my own office. Better yet, we could help each other start our own businesses.

27

Full of Beans

When my husband and I were newlyweds, living in our loft apartment across from a quickly-expanding mall area, I started writing about my work experiences, selling one such piece entitled, "I Have Seen the Future, and It's in Consulting" to the "From the Desk Of" opinion column of the *New York Times Money & Business* section.

In the mid-1990s infancy of the dot-com revolution, when we were still using CompuServe and a dial-up Internet connection, the closest I could get to the "gig economy" was to take a six-month assignment at a local insurance company creating databases or dashing between the IT and investment departments, translating needs and requirements so that projects could be completed on time.

After stashing those earnings away in our "house savings account" and paying off credit card bills, I would ditch my suits, briefcase, and nine-to-five schedule and don my alter ego "wife and writer" costume for a couple of months—running pants, tee shirts, and sneakers—and catch up on some of my fun creative projects.

The "dilemma" was that I would write an article in about twenty minutes, then spend the rest of the day on the cross-country ski machine, vacuuming the rug (again), watching the downstairs neighbor walk his cat on a leash every day at four p.m., and preparing midweek paella dinners with sangria, served on a vinyl tablecloth in our little dining nook. I was on a first-name basis with the mail carrier, and I watched the *Rosie O'Donnell Show*[3] every afternoon while polishing the stereo cabinet or color-coding the linen closet. One day Gray wrote, "Someone's been out of work too long" on a cartoon in which a wife reprimands her husband for putting the sweet relish with the 'r' rather than the 's' food in the alphabetized refrigerator.

One Saturday afternoon in January, Gray was downstairs, working on his master's thesis, when the phone rang up in the loft, where I had just completed a story for my writing class and was retyping my Rolodex and starting on next year's Christmas cards. To my surprise, it was a woman from a market research firm calling to ask me about my baked bean eating habits. Never before and never since that day has anyone except my mother ever expressed an interest in my preference for pinto vs. navy varieties, whether I felt I was getting adequate roughage in my diet, or if I had ever cooked my beanies with weenies. I considered myself a bean expert, since Mom made baked beans from scratch almost every Saturday night when I was growing up, soaking the beans the night before and then tossing in some onions and pork fat before dousing the whole vat in a river of molasses and tossing it in the oven to cook for the afternoon. Usually she'd serve a side of cheddar cheese "to complete the protein," along with a salad and some crusty bread. I had a very "regular" New England upbringing.

After half an hour, the bean lady admitted she had other calls to make but thanked me for my time and enthusiasm about her product and promised to send me a few bean coupon books in the mail. My husband took this moment to point out that this woman was actually the Universe telling me it was time for a new adventure. But

Full of Beans

when I evaluated new assignments, it seemed I had already "'bean' there, done that."

28

The Juggler

In 1990, the summer before my second year in the full-time M.B.A. program at the University of Connecticut, I was fortunate to obtain a spot in the summer leadership program at the international headquarters of the company where my father worked for over thirty years, Edifice Ascendoors. The three-storied, salmon-colored building lay at the end of a winding office park road surrounded by a shady walking trail, fragrant flower beds, and bushes sculpted into 'EA' logos. It had one-way tinted windows that offered its occupants a bird's-eye view of the sprawling parking lot, yet frustrated even the most determined sleuth (with binoculars) from catching a glimpse of operations behind its formidable facade.

The Juggler

I was looking forward to meeting fellow students and learning about their fields of study, as well as getting up to speed on the company's newest products and services and cutting-edge technology.

As a double major in Management Information Systems and International Business, I was particularly interested in how EA could control costs while maintaining productivity and customer satisfaction across its international divisions, while also keeping employees happy and being a good citizen of the earth and community.

Years later, a co-worker shared with me a snippet of Coca-Cola CEO Bryan Dyson's 1991 Georgia Tech commencement speech in which he compares life to juggling five balls in the air, namely "work, family, health, friends, and spirit," where work is a rubber ball that will bounce if dropped, and the rest are glass and will—well, I'd rather not find out.

But as a young professional investigating potential career "homes" for the next 30 years of my life, I was dying to know: how does an international corporation—like an individual—handle this challenging circus act? I figured that if I worked for a company that had its act together, with "nets" into which the glass balls might safely land if dropped, some of that magic might rub off on me, as well.

At the time, I was passionate about change agents—top executives hired to shake up major corporations, drilling down through layers of management to ferret out problems and implement creative solutions. I was excited to learn that EA's Chief Executive Officer, a wiry forty-something named Krill Kelprak, welcomed ideas from managers on down the line to people like me, twenty years before the *Undercover Boss*[71] reality TV show sent out top honchos—disguised in wild wigs, goofy goatees, and jumpsuits—to fling pizza dough, vacuum porta-potties, and stuff teddy bears. I couldn't wait to present my ideas to him and see if there might be a role for me to play at EA or its parent company, Unified Flibbetywickets Corporation (UFC). Dad would be so proud! We could have lunch together now and then, as his building was right down the lane.

I spent that summer ensconced in the carpeted, cooled partition village of EA's finance department, watching waves of numbers crash into each other before my bleary eyes and preparing fancy slides to summarize my recommendations at the Leadership Conference in August. It would have been nice to produce a slick animated slideshow on a laptop within minutes, or use a smartboard, but that technology was not yet available--we had only recently mastered walking upright and wearing high heels (though I still had trouble with that last one occasionally).

Our M.B.A. team enjoyed a picnic one beautiful evening, clustered around long tables in Mr. Kelprak's backyard while caterers scurried back and forth from his house with dishes and drinks. I met his lovely wife and well-mannered sons, stood in his immaculate kitchen, observed that his garage was bigger than my parents' first floor, and wondered how I came to be in that place.

The afternoon of my presentation, I arrived early and rehearsed my lines, double-and triple-checking my slides for errors and running to the ladies' room six or seven times. The chairs filled up, CEOs and CFOs in the first row, students and other headquarters personnel behind them, sipping ice water and tapping their pens on their notepads, some shrugging on jackets and straightening ties.

After a brief introduction—during which I struggled to breathe—I strode to the front, greeted the audience, placed my first slide on the glass, and flicked on the projector, not noticing the lamp was facing the audience, temporarily blinding the unfortunate President of EA's North American division—also known as My Father's Big Boss, Mr. Vandertwinkle—who happened to be sitting front and center.

After a pause, during which I scrambled to turn the projector, salvage what remained of my professional composure, and ignore the snickering of my fellow interns, "Mr. V" blinked, smiled at me, and said, "OK, you have my attention now!" I mumbled something about "shedding light on some issues" and completed my presentation, gratefully landing on my padded seat amid a ripple of laughter. Is it any wonder I managed to get another job in my life, with this tendency to turn into Lucille Ball whenever I found myself the center of attention? As it turned out, my UFC adventures were just beginning, in spite of—or perhaps because of—my desperate attempts to slip under the radar.

29

Inside Information

In the early 1990s, pursuing a career as a financial services sales representative with a local agency, I passed the standard licensing exams—Series 6, 63, and 7—which allowed me to offer clients insurance, annuities, and mutual funds in Connecticut, and started to call and meet with prospective customers.

As part of new agents' ongoing training, Buck Hyder, the firm's founder and Manager, administered a personality test designed to ferret out a few "producer" types, and relegate everyone else into a supporting role—lead generation, fact finding, or office support. Or so it always had done. Shaking his head in disbelief, Buck tested me twice.

It turned out I was both the Director, with an agenda and will to succeed (who "likes to run the show"), and the Counselor, a good listener who picks up all kinds of information about people.

At the beginning I was really excited, so I invited lots of people to seminars, got referrals, and even talked my friends into doing business with the firm. After unearthing clients' data--hopes and dreams, assets and liabilities, income and expenses--I'd often bring in a "power player" to close the sale, surrendering part of my commission.

It was a reasonable arrangement, considering I wasn't comfortable "moving in for the kill," especially if I'd been in people's homes, met their families, and knew they really didn't need—or couldn't afford--that snazzy variable-life insurance policy with all the bells and whistles. I needed to make a living, so I played the game.

For the top guys—four or five men with good hair, nice teeth, and impressive golf games--each sale meant a vacation, a car upgrade, a new suit. For me, each new client was an adventure, a chance to learn about people's lives legitimately, to share in them vicariously. I was building myself a sort of family, or community, in this pre-social media era. I envisioned becoming the boss of my own concern, where I shared information with people in order to help them and was compensated appropriately for my time and expertise.

After three years at the firm, I knew people flocked to Buck's weekly seminars at country clubs and hotels for the free munchies, a night out, and to bask in Buck's aura of confidence and success. They came to watch him pace the floor like a bulldog in shiny Italian loafers, shaking his fists and scolding, "If you fail to plan, you plan to fail!" (Benjamin Franklin)[72] and "If you don't know where you're going, you'll end up somewhere else!" (Yogi Berra)[73] At the end of the night, the attendees applauded heartily, scribbling their contact information on lists by the door as they left.

Buck promised a sense of protection, of complete control over adversity that, it turned out, couldn't be obtained from a monthly premium and an assortment of mutual funds, an annuity, or hot new bonds. Just like Dorothy and her ruby slippers in the *Wizard of Oz*[74]—who could have kicked her heels together and gone back to Kansas all along—the financially fitful carried a priceless treasure within them that was immune to the fickle fluctuations of health, financial markets, and public opinion.

Inside Information

At my last agency holiday party, in lieu of a bonus, gift certificate for a nice restaurant, or pricey bottle of wine, Buck presented me with a brown stoneware jug labeled "Inside Information." For a while, it sat on my desk, held my pens, and made me smile, to think that maybe Buck had finally figured me out, after all.

30

Bumpers and the Blarney Stone

Over the years, I constructed for myself an inverse relationship between acquiring knowledge and sharing it aloud with others. In school or at work, if I knew I was going to be called upon to introduce myself or do a presentation, I'd clench my fists and struggle to breathe, barely aware of what others were saying while I was mentally rehearsing my own lines. The more prepared I was, the more nervous I became that I might forget to say something important or be misunderstood.

Would I repeat something that someone else had said, or mispronounce a word or—worse—a name?

By the time my turn arrived I'd be a sweaty mess, hair damp on the back of my neck, my stomach churning.

While I dreaded speaking, I also dreaded that I couldn't *stop* myself from speaking once I saw that people were smiling and paying attention to me. The second situation was more dangerous, because of the adrenaline rush that accompanied it—like a tiny spark that quickly spread to a blaze.

From experience, I knew it was more likely that I'd get up there, stumble initially, then see a friendly face and proceed to ramble uncontrollably for half an hour about the evolution of the personal computer, how to prepare a New England boiled dinner, and how as a child I could beat everyone at Chinese Checkers—and still can—except for my dad.

The only thing that saved me from total humiliation was the same sense, presumably, that stopped the costumed roller-skating orangutan or the unicycling country singer (if such contestants existed) from continuing their act on the original 1970s *Gong Show*, hosted by Chuck Barris—a feeling that Corporal Klinger from *M*A*S*H* (actor Jamie Farr) was reaching for his mallet to strike the gong, and Phyllis Diller was itching to do the same. But I didn't just want to survive being gonged—I wanted to inspire and entertain. I wanted to engage and, as the old AT&T commercials urged us to do while I was growing up (in a campaign that would be flagged as scandalous and highly inappropriate today, despite simply meaning to warm someone's heart, or make them happy): "Reach out and touch someone."

To improve my public speaking ability I needed bumpers—those guides that my boys used when they were learning to bowl so the ball didn't drop into the gutter after meandering very slowly down the lane. Somewhere between reading an entire speech and completely "winging it" would be ideal—perhaps a few bulleted sentences to nudge me in the right direction, while I flowed with the energy of the room toward my goal of knocking down all the pins and leaving them laughing, or glowing, and wanting more.

I had an opportunity to speak up during my second year as a sort of perpetual intern (where I'd be on the payroll for 1,040 hours, then have to take three months off before returning) in the Commissioner's Office of the Connecticut Regulation of Energy and Protection of the Environment (CREPE). The agency was based in a six-story, red-roofed historic building overlooking Hartford's

Bushnell Park. Two golden angels flanked the steep steps leading to a massive front door, which took three people to heave open on a windy day (providing an impressive upper body workout).

Had I been a regular employee, I could have bypassed the 'visitors' entrance' and daily security vetting, slid my card through a reader, and snuck up the back steps or elevator in five minutes.

Although I lamented those things state employees enjoyed that I did not—outstanding benefits, job security, a salary (versus hourly pay), and educational reimbursement—I grew to appreciate certain advantages which my position afforded me, since I worked on the third floor, where decisions were made that trickled down to other bureaus, and ultimately, the good citizens of the state of Connecticut.

That St. Patrick's Day was a lucky one for me, as my supervisor, Morris—the Director of Communications—had allowed me to attend an Improvisational Communications class in the fifth floor auditorium, recently dedicated--with a special wall plaque--to former CREPE Commissioner "Geraldine 'Greenie' McEarthly,"[75] who was at that time serving as Administrator of the Environmental Protection

Agency (EPA) in Washington, D.C. About 20 agency employees, clutching reusable water bottles, took a well-deserved day off from saving the world from the effects of improper plastics disposal, blue algae blooming in streams, giant invasive weeds, destructive insects hitching rides on firewood, air pollution wafting toll-free through our state from the west and north, and black bears breaking down screen doors to steal brownies off kitchen counters, among other injustices and transgressions. All wore some shade of green—from olive to mint—except for one white-bearded guy from water permitting in his light blue short-sleeve shirt with the chest pocket.

Doreen O'Rally, the course instructor from the local community college, had us on our feet and away from our tables within minutes, introducing ourselves as if it were the first day of elementary school. Most were there to learn how to become more relaxed when speaking to the public on the phone or while giving presentations—not easy for scientists and engineers more comfortable hiding behind computers, in their cubicles. When it was my turn, I held back a bit, thinking my peers would question the need for a communications professional to take this course—after all, didn't I spend my days spreading information in various ways to the press, social media followers, and all manner of politicians, business leaders, and environmentalists? "Stand up straight, and project to the back of the room," Doreen barked at me while I was considering my defense. I lifted my chin and gazed north through the tall windows at the bare tree limbs whipping against the panes, the park beyond where gray squirrels scampered along the brown grass dotted with white hills of snow, then to the east, where earlier I'd noticed a few tender, green shoots poking their heads through the wood chips next to the "Smokey the Bear Fire Alert" sign. People smiled at me, perhaps enjoying having someone besides themselves in the hot seat. I realized they were actually cheering me on, rooting for me to look them in the eye rather than at the rhombuses repeating on the rug.

After lunch, when everyone had eaten and checked their e-mail, Doreen brought us all up onto the stage and handed each person a toy—red nose, orange lei, blue spinner, a horn—and told us to set up a work scenario involving one's personal "Blarney stone" and act out a story. When the shock wore off, one by one people came forward, using a purple Slinky™ to demonstrate municipal storm water runoff and a squeaky cow to describe composting. My new friend, "Sunny Bono"—a yellow smiling massage-ball figure with a tuxedo and white gloves—prompted me to explain what happens when the Communications department goes into crisis management mode, as it did that spring, when a mute swan protecting her nest scared two males in a kayak and had to be put down. I was so focused on Sunny that I didn't realize I'd shared information that folks in Wildlife knew but the Air and Water Bureaus didn't—a top-down, agency-wide perspective, from the intern. The Blarney stones had worked their magic, giving even the most reticent the ability to break through barriers. We gathered on the stage at the end for a group photo, still in character, for one afternoon not divided by bureau or title, but united in purpose: to share what each of us knows to improve our environment, our world, ourselves.

31

Fair Opal Starstamp

With all three of my astrological chart's work and resource houses –the second, sixth, and tenth—in water signs, is it any wonder my career has played out like a series of romantic comedies?

Each new cubicle became a cozy nook, co-workers my confidantes, the break room my personal kitchen, and—most dangerous of all—new bosses held the potential to be my intellectual inspiration, the vehicles through whom I would finally achieve my divine purpose in the world and be seen for precisely the person I aspire to be in my finest, shining moments.

Of course, my quixotic idealism set me up for failure. The "giant" injustices I charged toward—and heroically tried to 'slay'--were always windmills, the perfect "Dulcinea" bosses I placed on pedestals mere humans, and my reliable blue minivan—like the workhorse Rocinante—my powerful steed in which I traveled to my adventures. But--like Miguel de Cervantes' character Don Quixote,[76] the inspiration for *Man of La Mancha*[77]--I refused to see things for what they are, preferring instead to think some evil sorcerer had cast a transformative spell that altered their appearance.

While some people make wish lists for the perfect mate—smart, sense of humor, nice smile—I kept one in my heart for the perfect job: ten minutes from home, fun atmosphere, interesting people, the potential to learn and grow, and facilities enabling me to eat healthfully and get fresh air and exercise. In my mid-forties, having kissed several "frogs" on my way to career nirvana, I had spent the last eleven years freelance writing for the local newspaper from home while seeing my oldest son into sixth grade and the younger one into third, and had almost given up hope of finding my "prince" when I saw a "Career Fair" sign posted at the entrance of a town corporate park, practically in my neighborhood. Frustrated with dwindling assignments—and cash—from my editors and feeling increasingly out of place at morning "Mommy Zumba" at the YMCA, I dusted off my resume and e-mailed an application for a Marketing Associate in the nascent International Division of FlippetyDigital (FD), a local software firm. Then, I threw on a nice blouse and an old black skirt I had stashed in the back of the closet, hopped in my van, and delivered a copy in person, a practice that had always paid off for me in the days before heightened vigilance and electronic commerce.

I parked in the Visitors' area, my minivan—with its tiger paw magnet and honor roll stickers--towering above a sea of practical sedans and sleek crossover vehicles. Buoyed by that end-of-August, back-to-school yen to start something new (and need to escape the wilting heat into an air-conditioned oasis), I marched in, pleased to find my name on the list of interviewees. While waiting in line, I surveyed the crowd in the bright cafeteria, my stomach fluttering like a speed-dating contestant who has been out of the game for some time. Employees in black FD shirts and skinny jeans or leggings, clutching clipboards, darted back and forth as fast as possible in their flip-flops, managing the flow of traffic. Standing tall in my sensible black flats, I hugged my tote bag and realized I was probably in high school—or college--when most of these kids were born. In the midst of this reverie, a woman of about thirty with long, shiny black hair, wearing a navy blue and white polka dot dress—similar to a black and white one I'd worn in the mid-1980s with a chunky red necklace—walked toward me, stretching out her hand to shake mine. "Hi, I'm Opal Starstamp," she said. Unnerved by her sudden appearance, I began to blather in Spanish, as if I were talking to "la profesora" in my 9th grade Clase de Español. "¿Habla español?" Opal asked, to which I stammered "¡Claro!"—roughly, "Duh!"—as I had heard the man in front of me utter. She didn't seem to mind that my Spanish was a little rough, as I explained it had been twenty-plus years since I'd used it--while working for an international firm in Miami and, in the summer of 1985, as a college student living with a family in Madrid, Spain, immersing myself in the language and culture with a group of like-minded adventurers through a special University of Connecticut program.

In retrospect, the things Opal seemed to admire most in me at the beginning were the qualities that did me in, much like the "nice guy" you break up with for being wishy-washy. She admired my enthusiasm for the Spanish-language website she was developing to market U.S. cultural "experiences"—concerts, sports, and shows—to tourists from Mexico, Latin America, and Europe, and patiently answered my list of questions about the position and the team. She seemed wise beyond her years, someone who appreciated education, culture, and the finer things in life. I emerged from our short conversation heady with the excitement of a new venture, sensing a connection had been made--another chance to grab for that gold ring.

On the way out, after taking a multiple-choice test, I whipped out my flip phone to check in at home with my father-in-law, who was watching the boys, but a staffer cut me off, signaling they needed my attention elsewhere. I should have left then, gotten back onto my faithful steed and rode back to the hacienda to dream another day.

But there were windmills to slay, foreign customers' orders to fill, site traffic to analyze, English content to translate into Spanish. They created a special, 30-hour-a-week job for me, paid hourly with no benefits, so I could continue to volunteer teach religious education, go on the "Old Main Street" spring field trip, and have lunch at the middle school's 'soup bowls for hunger' fundraiser. I was living *my* dream.

Opal managed operations from her New York City apartment, training and evaluating us by phone, e-mail, and message throughout the day. The last Wednesday of the month, she'd rent a car and drive up for the day, eating with our little team in the cafeteria--which provided healthy, free meals to all employees--and allowing us to bask in the aura of her success for a short time, to keep us charged. She seemed to thrive on the change of scenery and freedom to come and go, but I sensed a distance between us growing with every visit. At the last holiday party I attended, FD CEO and founder Vic Bovini presented Opal with the "out of the box thinker" award, which she accepted graciously, thanking the team. Unfortunately, on her way back to the city, the award slipped out of its box onto the floor of her rental car, breaking into pieces. I would have preferred the "in the box" award, but it's the thought that counts.

Eventually, I added a few more hours to my schedule to support my family. That week, as Opal strode into the office, she greeted me with "So, how is the full-time employee AND full-time mommy doing?" in what I thought was her way of showing sincere concern but sounded to me like what you would say to a four-year-old who just figured out how to pat their head and rub their tummy at the same time. "Well, look at YOU, pulling all that off!" Meanwhile, I had been in a haze, feeling like Daniel (Robin Williams) in the restaurant scene of *Mrs. Doubtfire*,[78] where he scrambles between his latex-padded ladies' clothes and business suit to simultaneously meet with his boss about a new show and celebrate his ex-wife's birthday with their children and her new boyfriend.

Dashing between work and home so quickly, I was afraid someday I'd show up at the office in my work top and workout tights with my apron over them, not that anyone else would really notice.

At least I'd be wearing my fancy earrings and comfortable shoes, so I could work at my standing desk and then go for a walk, cape blowing in the wind.

32

Welcome to Room 125

January 3, 1980: from the diary of Zazoo Plazz, age 14

"Today Mr. Greer gave us this 'what have you done to show for your life' speech, which we were supposed to grip."

It was late August of 1979, and I could barely stomach my morning cereal, I was so anxious to start my freshman year at East Catholic High School, also called the "East Catholic Finishing School for Young Ladies and Gentlemen" by the Mangoes, a group of kindred souls a year my senior and therefore wiser in the ways of the world, at least upon their graduation in June 1982.

Welcome to Room 125

But I didn't have the benefit of their wisdom when I was selecting my blue plaid skirts, white blouses, and knee socks I would wear each day, choosing notebooks, pens, pencils, a lunch bag and backpack. I sprawled on a webbed aluminum lounge chair—the kind that left square marks on your sweaty, bare legs--losing myself in the first few pages of J. D. Salinger's *The Catcher in the Rye* while the Atlantic Rhythm Section's rendition of "Spooky" played on the radio and I invited the sun to kiss my face and knees so that I wouldn't have to show up pale the first week, with nothing to show for my summer at the pool and beach.

Though I had run the first day movie continuously in the multiplex of my mind for a week, entering the hallway of my first class with two minutes to spare felt like someone had fast-forwarded the tape so suddenly it was coming off the reel, twisting beyond repair, falling on the floor to be trampled like a neatly printed course schedule with a muddy size-eleven loafer stamped on its pristine face. Pressed to the wall as waves of students swept by, I fumbled with my locker combination, considering dashing into Room 125 for Literary Arts—honors English—with all my stuff, so to be on time. Yet the bell was ringing as I paused, the door closing, my future flashing before my eyes—failing English, summer school, my friends spending weekends with my parents at the Rhode Island beach house, sleeping in my bedroom, going for ice cream without me. Suddenly, my locker clicked open, allowing me to drop my backpack, grab my first period books, and slither into the room with my ears still ringing, heart pounding, and face flushed.

I had hoped to slide into a chair behind the teacher's back, but all but one desk in the middle were occupied, and so I found myself stranded in the front of the room, inspected from head to toe by my new classmates, some of whom had a "there by the grace of God, go I" look of relief on their faces.

The teacher, who introduced himself as Mr. Greer and—given his affinity for colorful plaid blazers--could have been the preppy understudy for Orson Welles, smiled like Sylvester the cat eyeing Tweety Bird in the cage as he interrupted his opening monologue, strolling over to me with his class list to ask my name.

My head started to throb as I replied and watched him run a chubby finger down the list. "What did you say your name was?" he asked. I repeated it, worrying now that I might indeed have gone to the wrong room, in which case I was even later for some other class. I glanced at my

Welcome to Room 125

schedule again, aware that the class was getting restless, sensing a scene was about to occur. I rocked from one foot to the other. The class knew I'd been late—why didn't he say something? The clock on the wall ticked for one, two minutes. Why was it so loud?

Finally I couldn't take it any longer. "I'm sorry I'm late," I stammered. "My locker wouldn't open, it's my first day, and I didn't know what to do!" When I'd finished, he turned to the class and said, "What do you think? Should we give her a break, just this once?" When no one objected, he revisited the list. "Oh! Here you are! I was looking on the wrong page!" I thought I saw a twinkle in his eye as I dropped into my seat.

Forty years later, I reflected on how fitting it was that the day I met the teacher who would challenge me to be "salt for the earth" and "light for the world" by pursuing a writing career would resemble a nightmare. (In fact, I often dream I'm running late for a class I can't find or walking into classrooms filled with teachers and students I don't know to take exams I must pass, years after obtaining my diplomas. My father *still* has those dreams, in his 80s.)

H. Allen Greer (1937-2005) was recognized as an Edgar Allan Poe Scholar, published in 1972. He introduced me to the macabre world of Poe and got me reading, at age 14, those poems and stories that would keep me awake at night, my imagination playing tricks on me as I saw shadows play across the ceiling. I think he saw in me—a Scorpio and fellow Poe aficionado-- someone who is fascinated by the concept of delving into the depths of the soul, relishing phrases such as "Presently I heard a slight groan, and I knew it was the groan of mortal terror."[79] (Poe, "The Tell-Tale Heart") This was Hitchcockian[80] terror-- fear that comes from our own imaginations--anticipated doom. I can't even look at a crow or raven without getting chills up my spine.

Mr. Greer had been teaching at East for about ten years when my class showed up, and already he was legendary. With degrees in English and Philosophy, he could have pursued a business career, become an author, or taught at one of those schools where vines crawled up the sides of the buildings and professors wore corduroy blazers with patches on the elbows and smoked tobacco in pipes while reciting Shakespeare. But the fact that he gave all that up to guide impressionable—and distractible-- young minds to appreciate and discuss novels such as John Knowles' *A Separate Peace* and Anthony Burgess's *A Clockwork Orange* leads me to believe that he followed St.

Welcome to Room 125

Paul's directive in his First Letter to the Corinthians, to "Strive eagerly for the greatest spiritual gifts."[81]

Ours was the first class of Generation X, spending afternoons at Computer Club, yet still cranking out most of our papers on typewriters, checking our grammar and punctuation in dog-eared copies of Kate Turabian's *A Manual for Writers*, turning in onion-skin-like pages with red margins, encasing them in colorful plastic covers with little plastic spines. My mom kept a few, mostly 'A' and 'A+' booklets from Mr. Greer's classes, his red comments scrawled diagonally across the back pages. It speaks volumes that she kept one physics paper on wind power and no math tests. But there was more to it than a high GPA--to get into his class you already showed by test scores and junior high grades that you were going places, or at least capable of doing so. Catholic school carried the onus of Luke's gospel:

"Much will be required of the person entrusted with much," and:

"Still more will be demanded of the person entrusted with more."[82]

I spent my best hours in Mr. Greer's Room 125--in class, homeroom, or as a staff member and senior co-editor of the literary magazine he moderated. Is it any wonder that I followed two red-haired classmates down that hallway at our 25th reunion to reminisce? The Holy Spirit called them individually to law school, to date and then marry, and volunteer their time and talent to those less fortunate. Once I decided to show up, the Spirit put me to work, too—waking everyone up, so they won't be late for school.

Happy 82nd Birthday, Mr. Greer.
4/30/19

33

Settle Down, Sally

From the Inbox of ZazooPlazz@home:

9/22/2016
To: ZP @ home
From: ElinorF @ StateCT

Hi Sally,

Good to hear your son got his learner's permit. So now you can tell him to go to Waterford to get a Nascar license. Sorry to hear your father-in-law is in the nursing home, is he OK with that? Yes, there was a bear near a school--I heard he was looking for you. Which race are you training to run? Sounds like you.

Settle Down, Sally

YES I WANT YOU TO COME BACK. October is two weeks away, 93 days until Christmas.

Nori Factsley

On my first day at the Connecticut Regulation of Energy and Protection of the Environment (CREPE), in early autumn, I wore my orange lizard-print wraparound top and brown pants with the shiny brown patent leather wedge heels and smiled widely for my official seasonal--or temporary--employee identification badge. I'm lucky it came out well, because they reused it over the next three years. I looked eternally youthful, yet woefully out of fashion within a short time—even more so, because I was wearing clothes I had bought at Suit Silo while working at FlippetyDigital, about three years before my CREPE adventures began. But I thought animal print was appropriate for working at a state agency charged with the protection of wildlife, and the sensible heels enabled me to navigate the rugged urban terrain over the mile walk from the employee lot. Within a week, however, I switched to slip-on sneakers in case I had to make a break for my car, given the rumors of muggings on the side street where I walked. Now that I think of it, I started running seriously while working at CREPE.

After getting my badge and lightly tussling with the accounting department over how much to withhold from my paycheck--an ongoing debate—I took the stairs to the third floor, home to the Chief of Staff, legal department, and Commissioner's Office to the east of the elevators and the water and land folks to the west. We shared restrooms and a kitchenette with some of those dam safety engineers, who were very good at their jobs, because for the most part the water stayed where it was supposed to be, unless somebody said to move it, and then they had to start all over again.

Morris, my supervisor, merited the largest office per his position as CREPE's Director of Communications. Across from Morris' office was a little carrel wedged between two larger cubicles and facing a laminated banner of the timeline of Connecticut's environmental movement over the past 40-plus years, beginning with the first Earth Day in 1970, followed by President Nixon's establishment of the Environmental Protection Agency.

Connecticut's environmental agency was up and running by 1971, just in time to address the pollution that was choking our air, filling our streams, and causing that

Settle Down, Sally

Native American man paddling his canoe through garbage to shed a tear in the public service announcement I had watched on television as a child. "Some people have a deep, abiding respect for the natural beauty of this country," said the announcer, accompanied by Western-movie music and drums, "and some people don't."[83] Later on, I discovered the marketing strategy behind that commercial, but the message had hit home, and apparently it was my turn to cry for Mother Earth, this time through Facebook posts, e-newsletters, and a sparsely attended electric vehicle charging station promotion (which, fortunately, was shown on local cable television or else it would have been held in vain).

As I lifted the cabinet door over my desk to put my lunch bag away, a large, black, hairy object with legs lunged toward me—a fake spider with realistic markings—and I jumped, despite having developed a high tolerance for such pranks as a 'boy mom'. My first thought was, "ooh, they got me good with that one," followed by, "who did that?" I suspected my neighbor, Elinor or 'Nori,' whom I'd observed enjoying her morning fruit salad, might be responsible. Cautiously, I opened a small drawer to my left and slid the pen compartment to the side to reveal a smug gray mouse. I picked it up by its rubber tail, walked to the first cubicle, and perched the mouse atop the monitor. Then I tiptoed back to my chair and waited. This person needed to know she was dealing with a Scorpio mom, not easily deterred from her work.

I borrowed eco-safe cleaner and brown paper towels from Jackie, the office manager, and cleaned my new space, making a mental note to bring those little fluffy duster refills for weekly touchups. I put up photos of my boys, some nature scenes, and a few funny magnets on the cabinets, and a small mirror so I could see who was about to sneak up behind me. Taking a sip of water from my reusable bottle, I smiled and settled in to tackle some e-mails.

Suddenly, I heard a raspy female voice behind me cackle, "Heh, heh, you found him, huh?" How had I not seen Nori in my feng shui mirror? Dressed in her Friday casual jeans and black and tan 'giraffe' sweater, with chin-length blonde hair feathered back into 'wings' favored by many late-1970s Charlie's Angels-in-training, she twirled the mouse around her finger and laughed so hard her face flushed pink, and I thought she was going to split her sides open. Noting her hawk-like eyes taking in my refurbished space, I pondered the fate of its previous occupant.

Settle Down, Sally

As the weeks wore on, I started wearing large, noise-cancelling headphones most of the day to compensate for the complete lack of privacy. Through the thin wall dividing us, I heard Nori pouring water from a jug into her cup—and then gulping it loudly--at least ten times a day. I heard nearly every word of every conversation she had, from "Hey, Ma!" at eight o'clock every morning to "Good afternoon!" to the guy who brought the newspapers just before lunch. But I also noticed that, in addition to being curious—or nosy, as I certainly can be—she was admirably stealthy. I'd walk to the break room and find her there, though I hadn't heard her leave. It was almost like working with my other half, like in that Discover card[84] TV commercial where a woman calls her credit card company and talks to her apparent twin, as the announcer crows: "We treat you like you'd treat you!"

The problem with using the headphones all the time was that I couldn't catch important conversations happening in 'command central'. Morris often called me in for a media phone call, to turn off (or on) some feature of a Microsoft Word document, or just to chat about the day's events. He didn't understand my need for quiet, and he wouldn't move Nori to the front desk because she couldn't answer the phones, do the fishing report, and submit the daily news bulletin when people were constantly bugging her. I compromised by wearing the headphones only when I needed to concentrate, usually after lunch when Morris went to the Capitol for meetings with the governor or was in front of the building talking to the local news stations about the latest environmental crisis.

Back then, eager to show my value in hopes of being hired for a full-time state position, I came in every day all gung ho to save the world and streamline the reporting systems, saving precious money and time. Nori, with almost 30 years at the state, would hear me getting all fired up—or receive one of my idealistic e-mails--and yell, "Settle Down, Sally!" Eventually, she started calling me Sally all the time. Our coworker Mindy, a friend from the YMCA who had referred me for the job, said, "How can you let her call you that?" But it really didn't matter, it was fun--and I knew that Nori had my back, after a while, because I started to have hers.

My first assignment was to compare offers from software firms promising to automate Nori's daily task of assimilating and distributing news stories of interest to the agency's employees. I whittled the field down to one company after Morris rejected the others' bids as too pricey for his budget. A salesman named Lance called and e-mailed me every day, hoping to win the state as a client with his fancy reports and notifications. Finally, I rolled his calls to Nori and sat down with my notepad and pen to find a sustainable alternative. In an hour, I devised a simple system using a popular note clipping application we already owned, which allowed Nori to save, format, and distribute the 'news clips' in a third of the time internally, requiring only that we subscribe to a few of the smaller publications that restricted access with firewalls.

Morris was thrilled to save thousands--and come across a hero to the Commissioner—as long as I could teach Nori to use the new system. He wondered what she would do with the time she used to spend copying, pasting, and complaining. I took the bull by the horns and told Lance we had found a less costly alternative. The following week he called to say he now worked for another firm. At this update, Nori yelled, "You drove him right over the edge, Sally!"

To bring Nori up to speed, I ended up writing detailed instructions, jumping up to help her every few minutes, and reassuring IT that I'd make sure she didn't blow up the entire database like she had last time. She eventually mastered it and did a pretty good job, except for those "Nascar Mondays" after a big race when she would call in 'sick'—or her cat was sick--and Jackie or I had to do the 'clips'. I didn't mind, but I yearned to write press releases, create digital publications, or ramp up the agency's GreenWreath Awards program, which gave free publicity, some mini Spanakopitas and little wooden plaques to firms the power companies had enticed to use newfangled energy efficient lightbulbs, or people who had become obsessed with making little stinky piles of orange rinds and tea bags and yelling at those who threw yogurt containers into the wrong bin in the break room. Much as Nori sometimes tried my patience with technical matters, she ran rings around me when it came to answering the phones, listening to people scream about the bear, fox, or raccoon rummaging through their trash, and driving Morris up the wall several times a day.

Given that Nori was apt to tailgate the Grim Reaper, I shouldn't have been surprised to learn she was a Scorpio, her November birthday falling a few days after mine. She was the cool big sister I'd never had, a fellow 'Pluto in Virgo generation' middle child stuck between the elder Pluto in Leo Boomers and younger Pluto in Libra kids. I'll bet she hung her dolls by their hair in a tree as I did, taking photos of Mrs. Beasley—the blonde, blue-eyed, bespectacled doll from *A Family Affair*[85]-- in various awkward positions, just to stir the pot.

    Nori preferred celebrating other people's birthdays to her own. She shunned sugar and regifted balloons, but on my third birthday at the agency, I walked into my window-lit office to find a beautiful autumn bouquet and a tray of six chocolate 'mud' cups riddled with multicolored gummy worms. The card--perched on a stick topped by a grinning scarecrow--read: "Surprise! Happy Birthday, Sally!"

10/6/2016
To: ZP @ home
From: ElinorF @ StateCT

Hi Sally,

Are you all set for the Hartford Marathon this weekend? I was asking Morris when you can come back…
    I forgot how to archive the articles… Really.

Nori Factsley

34

Uncle Mabel Anger

"There is a time to laugh and a time not to laugh, and this is not one of them."
Inspector Jacques Clouseau,
from *Inspector Clouseau*(1968)

The photo--taken in May of 1987 at the surprise college graduation party my parents threw me at a restaurant in Glastonbury, Connecticut—says it all. Uncle Moe is holding the microphone, giving a speech in my honor.

Tall and trim, dressed impeccably in crisp black slacks, a pale blue shirt, yellow tie, and dark mauve jacket, rose tinted glasses perched on his regal nose, and a sprinkling of salt in his dark hair and moustache, he looks like he would be just as comfortable addressing a conference room of insurance salespeople at the annual Pebble Beach bash as a couple dozen of our closest friends and relatives in a back room at the Cellarie, where my friends and I went to dance many Saturday nights.

To Moe's right, Aunt "Olivienne," or "Liv," stylish in a summery pink dress trimmed in white with a black bow, her black pixie cut highlighting her high cheek bones and long neck, rests her elbow on the table, the long fingers of her left hand cradling her chin as her eyeballs roll skyward behind her tinted glasses like the angel in the print of Raphael's cherubim of the *Sistine Madonna* that Gray and I bought for our first apartment (which still hangs over our couch). But Liv is looking away from Moe, perhaps a knee-jerk reaction to one of her brother's coarse jokes. At Moe's left, Bunny seems to be enjoying herself immensely while crushing her cigarette in an ash tray. Uncle "Ronnie," Liv's husband, sporting a dark tan and tasteful summer whites with a pale pink tie perfectly matched to his wife's dress, smiles down at his empty coffee cup as if he is wondering, "When will Moe be done so we can eat the cake?"

A copy of Moe's speech, on thick, cream-colored paper, falls out of the back of the yellowing album where two dozen photos are stuck forever, sealed in plastic.

Reading his words, I am, once again, that "roly-poly, chubby" two-year-old whose best effort at pronouncing her full name was—to Moe's great amusement—'Essie Bidowe,' and 'Essie' I would remain, despite becoming "a good looking, long drink of water" and college graduate. I was blushing and trying to hide under the table when he spoke these words, so they never properly sunk in until now, as I ready for the next phase of my life.

I imagine greeting him one day in the spirit realm where he now resides, tilting my head upward to regard his over-six-foot-tall presence, standing on tiptoe to give him a hug, and frantically trying to think of something clever and grown-up to say, as he kisses my cheek, calls out "Hiya, Essie!" and offers me a Shirley Temple with extra maraschino cherries and a little umbrella stirrer. I picture him floating around the clouded streets in a big American car, his license plate "AWCMON" betraying his frustration at celestial construction or that St. Peter's clubhouse wasn't available for next Tuesday's Rotary Club meeting. Perhaps he is lost there without Bunny to challenge him on politics—he was a lifelong Democrat, she a staunch Republican—or play 'devil's advocate.' No one laughed harder than Bunny the day he received an envelope addressed not to his legal name—M. A. Belanger—but to 'Mabel Anger.'

With his signature dark glasses, prominent nose, and ubiquitous moustache, he looked like a cross between Vince Guaraldi, the jazz pianist who performed the soundtrack for Charles Schultz' *Peanuts* animated specials, and actor Peter Sellers of the *Pink Panther* movies from the 1960s and '70s. My dad once dared to don a fake nose/moustache combo for a laugh, demoting himself a peg or two in Moe's opinion but clearly enjoying himself despite—or because of—that reaction.

I'd hoped Moe would launch into an impression at the party, as he often did at family gatherings, but it was neither the time nor place. Watching the *Pink Panther* movies starring British actor Peter Sellers (which gave rise to Uncle Moe's perfect moustachioed, trenchcoated "Inspector Clouseau" faux French impression, "Waiter, there is a bimp in ma sip!"), I realized that Uncle Moe really had some acting chops, since he was a French Canadian-American man playing a British man pretending to be a French man.

What Moe chose to do on this occasion was entertain the crowd while making me confront myself, and what I wanted from life. Saying my Bachelor of Science degree in

Finance from Boston College would be "good training to raise a houseful of kids and balance the family budget" and "will guide your career as much as my English degree helped me to become a conference and travel planner" threw me for a loop, given my recent decision to return home to Connecticut and pursue a career in investments. "Frankly," he continued, "exposure to your college roommates probably did you more good than your education."

Then he reassured me that, though I'd left the "culture, fun and sophistication of Boston," our "fun city" east of Hartford offered "gourmet restaurants like Augie and Ray's drive-in, plenty of education resources such as our two adult bookstores, and the epitome of culture, the (topless strip club) Pompeii Café." But as a redevelopment commissioner, he had big plans for the town, and today most of the dancers wear tops. He also had a role in persuading the owners of a monstrous black-paned building by the river—which he dubbed "the Darth Vader building"—to paint it gray, just in time for me to apply for a job there. "At least you'd be looking out, rather than *at* the building," he reasoned.

There's one photo I missed, tacked onto the last page. I gaze upward, bright-eyed and clad head-to-toe in white, save for a turquoise necklace and earrings, hot pink lipstick and a mop of brown curls. Uncle Moe points his index finger at me like Monty Python's "Hand of God" coming down from the clouds, as Mom looks on. Perhaps he is scolding me for "not having the decency to become Mrs. Doug Flutie (BC's Heisman trophy-winning quarterback)" after my parents spent a fortune on my tuition.

"Regardless," he said in closing, "I want to welcome you to the real world, Leslie…we're waiting for you!"

35

Leo Joseph and the Eight-Sided Table

My parents' idea of a fun Sunday, from the time I was able to sit by myself in the back seat of the car (sans seat belt), was to go hunting for antiques somewhere in Connecticut. They particularly admired early American colonial pieces—tables, chairs, spinning wheels, hutches, and clocks—even if they were broken, stained, dusty, smelly, or really, really, old.

To my uninitiated senses, most of the junk we saw fell into all of those categories. But they knew what they were looking for, and occasionally adopted a forlorn footstool or creaky clock.

When we got home, the real magic would happen, as Dad carefully laid the item on the slab of newspaper covering his gray workbench in the basement, rolled up his denim sleeves, adjusted his safety glasses, and commenced

Leo Joseph and the Eight-Sided Table

surgery. I would sit on the cellar stairs in the dark--far enough away not to choke on the sawdust storm or get giddy on varnish vapors—and watch him lose track of time in his determination to uncover the swan hidden beneath each ugly duckling. Judging from the dozen or so clocks (set to various times) and solid, well-polished furniture still in my parents' home to this day, this process went beyond a hobby to something that has enhanced and sustained their 60-year marriage.

So it was that, in addition to having a foundation of modern, functional furniture in our house—bedroom sets, couches, and armchairs—we always had a few items sprinkled here and there that had stories. There was the coffee table into which I (Zazoo) gleefully sunk my baby incisors while teething. Mom is proud to point out the beautifully preserved bluish gray chair she inherited from her grandfather Florian St. Laurent's early-twentieth-century ice cream parlor in Fall River, Massachusetts. Nobody ever dared sit on it, perched as it was on the upstairs landing with a basket of dried flowers for company. Though I never knew my great-grandfather, I do wonder how much his chair would fetch online.

I did my homework on a narrow desk that matched my bedroom set. It suited me until middle school, when I couldn't fit my long legs under it, or my books on top. Somehow it trailed me until 2010, when I encouraged my seven-year-old son to conduct science experiments on it in the hopes that we would be unable to remove the green goo from its tired bronze handles. Ultimately—I figured—it would land at the curb for the local "junk guy" to pick up in the middle of the night. To my dismay, the kid insisted on studying at—and cramming all kinds of "treasures" into—that desk until 2017, when he started high school and switched to a modular computer desk with ample room for legs and books. The old desk, now in the upstairs hallway, mocks me with its usefulness, providing a safe nook for the doggie bed as well as a storage area for baby books and photo albums. "It needs a good sanding and a new coat of paint, some snazzy drawer pulls," I think as I pass by.

Adopting items that once belonged to someone else always seemed risky to me, particularly if the previous owner's spirit accompanies them at no extra charge. There's no telling what's swirling around in there. But if you are fortunate enough to receive useful items from beloved relatives' estates, it's like a "zap," a little charge from above, reminding you to carry the family torch proudly, to smile, and to dust regularly. One such piece is my maternal grandfather's maple octagonal table, one of a pair that flanked his sturdy "Papa Bear" rocking chair by the front window of the little Cape he shared with my grandmother for forty years. Memere passed away in 1982, leaving him to rock alone next to the empty "Mama Bear" chair until he joined her in 1985.

The tables fell through the cracks somehow, as the heirs and lawyers settled the estate and divided the insurance proceeds. To one child went the good china, to another the cameo ring, a few photos and knickknacks, the detritus of a fifty-five-year marriage. Memere's table sits by Mom's bed, holding her astrology magazines, the phone, a lamp, a cross and sacred prayer cards. Pepere's table--soiled and faded from its former 1950s Sears catalogue luster--sulked in a corner of our basement until two summers ago, when I took it upon myself to rejuvenate it in time for my oldest son's 17th birthday in September. I thought Bren should inherit something that had belonged to his great-grandfather Leo Joseph--whom he had never met—besides his middle name.

Pepere watches me open a gift from his favorite chair on Christmas night, 1967.

Leo Joseph and the Eight-Sided Table

I had never undertaken a staining project like this on my own, without help from Dad or Gray, but after reviewing a hundred videos and websites on "wood restoration projects," I drove down to the mega-hardware store, grabbed an orange cart, and put myself at the mercy of an "expert" who set me up with everything I needed (and about $50 worth of stuff I could have done without). One hot Sunday afternoon while the guys were at Boy Scout camp, I unscrewed the legs of the table, removed the black metal arrows screwed to four sides, and rested the hollow trunk on an old sheet in the garage.

Squatting on a plastic bench in shorts, an old tee shirt, plastic gloves, safety glasses, and a mask, I started sanding off the top surface—scruff, scruff, scruff-- as the neighbors strolled past with their dogs and strained to see what the heck I was "up to" this week. As I sanded, I could almost smell Pepere's cigar resting in its metal ashtray, and see a dish of cashews, our favorite snack. He mastered 'the scoop,' whereby he daintily selected one or two nuts between thumb and forefinger while excavating two-thirds of the contents of the bowl with the lower three fingers so quickly that no one—or so he thought—was the wiser. I knew his little tricks, and I also knew that Memere hid the 'ninnons' (her French-Canadian word for chocolates) where she thought he wouldn't find them, like under the towels in the linen closet. But somehow he always found them, and she had to find a new hiding place.

When I finished sanding the top, I stood to sweep up the debris and admire the beautiful wood grain emerging beneath. Judging from the elbow grease I had applied to reveal it, I figured someone had slapped on an extra coat or two of stain in an attempt to improve its appearance. The next couple of Sundays I sanded the sides and lower level, craning my neck to remove stubborn strips concealed in the corners. At this point I was one with the table, patiently coaxing it to reveal its potential. In its old life, it had held a stack of *Field and Stream* magazines whose covers boasted "Big Trout!" and "Stripers." I'd never seen Pepere happier than the time he took me fishing in his little rowboat, cigar nub perched on his lips, a few feathery flies on his tattered tan hat. The boat nearly toppled from a cooler full of food, much more than we needed.

I'd slapped on a sealant and one coat of Early American oak stain when my parents stopped by for a visit one Sunday afternoon in late August. Glancing at my makeshift workshop, Dad remarked that he "would have used the water-based stain" for easier cleanup and lower

Leo Joseph and the Eight-Sided Table

fumes. They sped off to the mall, leaving me in the garage to add another coat while I recalled scurrying to turn on the TV Sunday nights after dinner in the 1970s so Pepere could watch *All in the Family* and smile as Archie Bunker (Carroll O'Connor) squabbled with his "Dingbat" wife, Edith (Jean Stapleton) and liberal son-in-law, Michael "Meathead" Stivic (Rob Reiner). "Those were the days," indeed.

    I applied the last coat of varnish in late October, picking out the dead pine needles the wind had blown onto the table's pristine facade. I admired my work and took a few photos before stowing my tools in an old trash can for future projects. Two days later, I saw the 'gift' nestled between Bren's bed and desk, underneath his junior black belt designation. "Thanks," he said, turning his head to look at me a second before resuming his computer game. Glancing at the lamp, tissues, and cell phone above deck, college brochures and *Walking Dead* comics below, I smiled and closed the door. "He may have inherited the table," I thought, "but the cashews are all mine."

Leslie B. Placzek / Adventures of Zazoo Plazz

The refurbished table, in Brenin Joseph's room.

36

Zazoo Plazz, Zealous Performer

When we had relatives over for holiday dinners or other special occasions, everyone had a job. Mom cooked and served the dinner and decorated the table. Dad was in charge of greeting people at the door, taking their coats, settling them in the living room, and distributing drinks and appetizers. After dessert, it was my turn to entertain everyone by telling a story, tap dancing, or banging out a tune on the keys of the top-of-the-line mid-1970s Hammond organ that occupied half of the dining room. Sometimes Dad joined me on the saxophone or clarinet, but usually I was on my own, taking requests and sprinkling in a few of my tried-and-true favorites that always garnered applause.

Zazoo Plazz, Zealous Performer

Pepere—Mom's father—would settle into his favorite armchair in the far corner of the living room, the one upholstered with little squares of red and orange bouquets and colonial scenes, that no one else ever dared sit in while he was present. From there he could watch me play the organ and call out to me to play "Moon River" or "Red River Valley," among other schmaltzy tunes from long ago that must have struck a chord with him, because he'd dab at his eyes and stare off into space. I never asked if it made him happy or sad—I just kept playing.

Sitting tall on the padded black leather bench of that Hammond organ gave me an illusion of command over my world comparable only to sitting at the wheel of my minivan or perching on the chartreuse exercise disk at my dining room 'desk,' where I pedal my elliptical trainer while typing these words on my ergonomic keyboard. Pressing the 'on' button, I felt the organ whir to life beneath my hands, heard it hum like a spaceship preparing for takeoff into outer space. I pushed and pulled black and white levers to get the perfect sound, engaging the built-in Leslie speakers that I always thought were named for me rather than for some guy named Donald Leslie,[86] who invented them in the 1940s to bring the acoustics of a cathedral to the suburban living room. I didn't really know what any of the knobs were—I just fiddled with them until I found a sound I liked that day. Sometimes I experimented with the rhythm buttons—cha-cha-cha, rock, jazz—just to rock the boat. When everything was beeping and flashing, I'd launch into my first song as if I were Star Wars' Han Solo (played by Harrison Ford) rocketing the Millennium Falcon into the galaxy, Chewbacca by his side. May the musical "force" be with us!

I learned to play the organ at age seven, after a few embarrassing dance recital moments and clumsy practice sessions led my parents to concede I was never going to be the next Shirley Temple or a *Chorus Line* dancer on Broadway. Every Wednesday after school, Mom drove me to my organ lesson in her boxy, four-door, turnip-colored 1970 Datsun 510—a model I called "the tangerine machine" and the auto industry nicknamed "the bluebird" or "poor man's BMW."[87] If I dialed the finicky a.m. radio just right, we could pick up the Carpenters crooning "We've Only Just Begun" as we traversed the bumpy highway eastward to the Downtown Manchester exit. I was excited to embark on this musical adventure and add a new skill to my repertoire.

Zazoo Plazz, Zealous Performer

The Watkins organ and piano studio, just off Main Street in Manchester, Connecticut, was ninety percent furniture emporium and ten percent musical prodigy training center. The booth where Mrs. Marjorie Metronome taught lessons overlooked the sales floor, where a variety of keyboards encased in highly polished cabinets awaited adoption by musical amateurs blessed with free time and large living spaces.

I'd heard Mom play the small spinet organ at home, cautiously making her way through "I Beg Your Pardon (I Never Promised You a Rose Garden)" so as to hit all the right notes.

It seemed like hard work, but "Marge," a well-known local church organist and keyboard instructor, made it look almost effortless. Dressed in tailored skirts or slacks and blouses, her dark hair swooping up and away from her forehead, Marge looked like a modern businesswoman as she approached the organ bench and settled herself to play. The organ seemed to stand at attention as she donned her glasses, glanced at the music, and inhaled deeply, rolling her shoulders back as if opening her heart to receive the notes. As her fingers descended upon the keys, and her feet hit the pedals, her body moved with the beat of the song like a boat bobbing on the waves.

At home, my friends and family giggled as I bounced on the bench like Marge to a peppy song. It was hard to get a good bounce going with so little natural padding.

By the spring of that first year of lessons, Marge invited me to play a couple of songs at the annual Hammond Organ Society concert, held in the showroom with punch and cookies served afterward. If I was nervous when I first started, it wore off after the first song in my set, as people started smiling and clapping. I wondered if anyone bought an organ after the concert. Did I earn any commission?

One December, I sat at an organ in Watkins' front window, playing Christmas carols that were piped outside. Carols were simple and fun to play--not that anyone was going to criticize an eight-year-old in a long red plaid skirt, prim white blouse, short wavy brown hair, and oversized eyeglasses pounding out "Deck the Halls" on a double-decker keyboard while straining to touch the pedals with the tips of her patent leather shoes. Marge stood close by, monitoring the equipment and making sure I didn't slide off the bench or lose my place. Mom—my agent--stood on

Zazoo Plazz, Zealous Performer

the sidewalk, informing passersby, "That's my daughter playing in there!"

The other day, I was flipping through my organ music collection and happened to open a Scott Joplin ragtime book to the first song, "The Entertainer," popularized in the Oscar-winning 1973 movie *The Sting*. At the top, Marge had penciled in the date--April 3, 1978—and double-underlined the tempo, "Not fast." Here and there, she had circled a tricky note, reminded me to play "one octave higher," and highlighted a pedal note I tended to skip over repeatedly, figuring no one would really notice, anyway. "Count," she urged, numbering a series of descending flats. Marge's notes—and passion for performing—urge me, even now, to temper my wild, pre-adolescent enthusiasm for music with the discipline of a master keyboardist.

Though the Watkins Wednesdays eventually yielded to high school activities, social life, and banjo lessons, I continued to play the organ on weekends and special occasions through college. Rather than buy new music, replacing the disco hits compilations with my favorite Billy Joel hits, I played "The Entertainer" over and over, trying to improve each time. If Pepere grew as tired of this as I did, he never said a word, just nodded and tapped his foot from his favorite spot in the corner of the room.

37

The Banjo Nose Best

"You can't play a sad song on the banjo--it always comes out so cheerful."
- Steve Martin, comedian and banjo player

When I was in middle school, I got a hankering to pick and strum the five-string banjo. Perhaps this arose from all the Saturday nights I'd sat in the den watching *Hee Haw*, a country version of *Laugh-In*. I recall the girls in gingham miniskirts, crop tops, and pigtails trading jokes in the cornfields with goofy guys in overalls, Grandpa Jones promoting pork and beans with cornbread for supper ("Yuuum, yum!"), and Minnie Pearl--in her signature square-necked blue dress and flowery hat with its flyaway price tag—hollering "Howdee!" at the gang, Grand Ole Opry-style.

The Banjo Nose Best

But what drew me to *Hee Haw*, and fueled my feverish banjo fixation, was the mischievous twinkle that appeared in Roy Clark's eyes as he launched into "Dueling Banjos"[88] on his five-string alongside a guest, both musicians' fingers building up speed until they seemed to set off sparks, seemingly effortlessly--yet joyfully--filling the air with high-pitched twanging as the cast stomped, clapped, and yelled, "Yahoo!"

I must have made a convincing argument, since Dad bought me a real five-string banjo with an embroidered strap, carrying case, and a bunch of music, including a collection of John Denver's greatest hits and the banjo beginner's bible, *Earl Scruggs and the 5-String Banjo*. He seemed happy to encourage my slightest interest in music, despite my complete failure to master the entire family of reed instruments (saliva-challenged as I was), the harmonica, tambourine, and kazoo. He'd probably already made his peace with the fact that demand for bluegrass performers in Connecticut was dismal, and we weren't moving to Nashville, so there was little possibility of a banjo scholarship for college.

If I had thought this through a bit more, I could have avoided those finger calluses, but then I would have missed out on the adventures. I may not yet have been south or west of Pennsylvania, but I was hoping the music would transport me, move my soul in new--yet familiar-- ways. As John Denver sang, "Take Me Home, Country Roads."[89]

For a year or two, I took both organ and banjo lessons. My first banjo lesson was with Roland Kord, an older gentleman reputed to have played banjo with Earl Scruggs, the North Carolinian and Bluegrass Hall of Famer credited with mastering the three-finger banjo picking technique. When Dad dropped me off one afternoon at "The Banjo Man's" basement studio, though, I was overcome by the smell of his pain ointment and couldn't concentrate on the lesson. It was a shame that I couldn't get past it, because the guy was so good, Dad said it was "like pulling teeth" to get an appointment with him at all.

Next, my folks lined up a local instructor, "Big Louie" Odorosa, who came to our house with his guitar every week for a couple of years and taught me to play, if not remotely like Roy Clark, at least as well as could be expected with my chunky fingers, which frequently frustrated my fretting up and down the narrow neck. We would sit side by side in the dining room, Louie strumming the guitar part of "Cripple Creek" as I picked along happily on the banjo. The only problem was that every time he left, Mom started flinging open the windows and spraying Lysol® all over the room. Then she rotated the chair cushions and threw the one he'd used in the wash, without saying a word. This went on for some time, until she finally tossed the cushions and poor Louie almost slid off the highly waxed chair onto the braided rug. I thought all this could have been avoided if we had played outside somewhere, like on a wraparound porch out in the country, with a nice, cold glass of lemonade afterward.

The biggest advantage the banjo had over the organ was its portability. I could toss the case into the car with my music and play on the weekend down at my family's summer cottage on the south shore of Rhode Island, often with friends accompanying me on their guitars. With little to distract me except the sun, sea breeze, and waves, I could relax and learn to play a new song or incorporate a useful tip from a fellow strummer on how to hold the neck, tune, or play more complex combinations.

Leslie B. Placzek / Adventures of Zazoo Plazz

The Banjo Nose Best

The banjo was with me, more so than the organ, until my late twenties, when I got married and moved into an apartment (where thin walls discouraged me from jamming "Foggy Mountain Breakdown" at full volume at 10 p.m.). I bequeathed it to my father, who shoved it in the cellar next to my baby doll crib and antique student desk. It sat there for twenty years, redolent with the scent of mothballs. One mid-November day in 2018, I settled in at my laptop to write and up popped the news that Roy Clark, legendary guitarist, Country Music Hall of Famer, multiple award winner, and Grand Ole Opry member, had died of pneumonia at age 85. Of course, the article continued, he was best known as co-host of the *Hee-Haw* television series. The country roads took Roy home. A few months later, I drove over to my folks' house and brought my banjo home, to its rightful place by my side. (Two weeks after that, Jack broke it while showing off to his friends, and I had to take it to the guitar store for repairs).

38

The Aquarian Centenarian

Recently, my paternal cousin Nate saw a photo of me on Facebook and remarked that I "resembled our Granny" in her younger days, admitting that, in middle age, he had inherited "Grandpa Bilodeau's receding hairline." I owned up to having Granny's tiny teeth, light brown, flyaway hair, and a variety of brown moles (my "beauty spots," lovingly called "zin zins") sprinkled liberally over my face and body. Though I removed the largest moles, including one on the right side of my face, I've come to terms with the fact that the "French freckles" are here to stay. Granny seemed to get more moles as she grew older, either as points for good behavior or from careless exposure to the unforgiving rays of the sun.

The Aquarian Centenarian

At the end of her long life--one month shy of her 103rd birthday—I imagine her skin must have appeared, to my four-year-old son sitting on her lap, like chocolate chip cookie dough. This got me thinking about how I had Granny in my life for almost 40 years—20 years longer than my other grandparents--and what that said about her, as well as about myself as a "'Za-zin' off the ol' mole."

Leona Saucier Bilodeau was born on January 26th, when the sun was in Aquarius, the second-to-last sign of the astrological year. I learned a lot about Aquarians—and longevity—by hanging out with Granny, and I treasured these observations—stored them deep in the cedar hope chest of my heart-- to share them someday with others who might benefit from hearing about her amazing adventures, quirky observations, and unique creations in this earthly realm.

The sunny kitchen of Granny's yellow cape was full of plants. Some she admired for their flowers, some kept her company, and some she ate or used medicinally, like the pots of herbs on her windowsill (at least, I thought they were herbs). She ate more plants than animals as she advanced in years, but her diet seemed to change radically each time she ate at our house. One holiday, Mom served her a nice baked chicken dinner, at which point Granny looked down at her plate and said, "Well, I really don't eat meat anymore, I eat fish." Then Mom bolted out of her chair, frantically searching the cupboards for a can of tuna fish to serve her mother-in-law. Granny would smile just the tiniest bit, her little teeth showing, and sigh, "Oh, don't fuss, I'll just eat the potatoes and green beans. I'm not that hungry, anyway." Then she insisted on pouring hot sauce over whatever she ate, which may have contributed to her lengthy lifespan. Like a bird, Granny mostly subsisted on fruit and nuts, and by age ninety she ate just vegetables and pie.

Granny made the best lemon meringue pie I have ever tasted, whipping the white topping perfectly so it floated like a fluffy cloud over the sunny pool beneath it. This is not a talent I inherited, given the four Easters my mother had to pick up last-minute pies at the store to replace the soggy, lemon-scented messes sinking to the bottom of my trash can. I don't remember eating many meals at Granny's, but who cares, when there's pie? We always seemed to visit when she had just dropped off a fresh batch of cookies at my aunt's house for my cousins to enjoy. Either my timing was terrible, or she wanted to teach me about the joys of charity, the character-building nature of self-discipline, and how envy makes you hungry.

Over the years, I've had glimpses of Granny in the way my thumb and forefinger grasp a book or newspaper, the slope of my knuckle while buttoning one of my sons' coats when they were small, just as she may have done Dad's. I remember clearly the way she would stand, or sit, and just stare at me after we'd hugged 'hello' or 'goodbye,' her eyes behind thick lenses looking me up, down, and up again, while her hands smoothed her skirt, or searched for a pocket, looking for a way to be useful while the rest of her was socializing. In her last years, she would turn her hearing aid off, or low, if she wanted to tune out ambient noise in the nursing home, causing her to say, "Eh?" a lot. This reminded me of how Dad would always take off his glasses at the dinner table and rub his eyes before eating, to give that sense a break while the other ones were in use. Sometimes he ended up with his nose in the mashed potatoes.

There are so many questions I would ask Granny today, like about her childhood experiences as a homesteader, compared to those Laura Ingalls Wilder wrote of in her *Little House on the Prairie* books, later made into a popular 1970s TV show. I stare at photos of Granny on Christmas--sporting her black and white tweed suit with the red blouse tied at the neck, hands clasped in her lap or at her sides—and feel grateful for all the holidays we shared, her support for my dreams, the afghans she knitted for my bed. From her birth in 1902 in a sod house bordering the Sioux Reservation in South Dakota to parents of French-Canadian descent to her last breath on Christmas morning of 2004, she was a pioneer, the solid branch from which so many twigs sprouted and have borne fruit or will do so in the future.

Like drawing a map from one 'zin zin' to another on my skin to see the big picture, I strive to connect the clues Granny left me about her own life. Sometimes, when the Aquarius moon rises in the night sky, I imagine my moles are lit from within like the pegs stuck in a Lite-Brite screen from my Zazoo years, illuminating the path I will forge and the life I will create in my second half-century.

The Aquarian Centenarian

EPILOGUE

Doggie Drama--and Dharma

My dog Bebe rarely barks without a good reason—the Bus o' Sprouts has arrived with the groceries, Charlie the Cockapoo is outside with his mom (again), or I am trying to enjoy a hug or conversation with my husband in which she is not included. When the shadows (and her growling stomach) tell her it's dinnertime, she calmly trots to her stainless dish and flips it with her paw once, twice, or as many times as is necessary until we stop what we are doing and toss in a scoop of her favorite chow. Each time she exerts additional energy until she flips it over into her water dish or scrapes it along the floor with her nose until it nudges the closet where we store the food container.

My mother tells me that as a baby, I employed similar tactics as my dog to get my point across. One morning at breakfast, she handed me a bottle of milk and turned away, only to feel the rush of air by her ear, seconds later, as I threw the bottle across the kitchen from my playpen with such force I nearly knocked her over. "I figured you were ready to drink from a cup," she said. So I did, quite happily.

When I take Detective Dog for a stroll around the block, she holds her head up high, wagging her tail from right to left, right to left, until she smells something interesting, at which point she yanks with the considerable strength of her Jack Russell Terrier torso and legs until I am flying across the grass, coming to rest where her pointy Labrador Retriever nose has found an interesting spot, perhaps among some rabbit droppings or first grader's discarded bread crusts in a plastic bag strewn on the side of the road. She follows her nose for a few yards, zigzagging from sidewalk to woods, until she finds an appropriate place to eliminate, kicking grass over it until I am brushing dirt from my sneakers, annoyed that I allowed myself to be used in such a fashion. Wrapping the leash several times around my hand, I say, "Okay, missy, let's run!" and we sprint home, Dubious Dog glancing at me sideways now and then to gauge my mood: "Will we take the long Sunday route (where lots of dogs live) or the short weekday one?" When we get home and remove her leash, the Detached Dog usually tears around the living room for a while until she gets tired, then curls up on the couch for a rest, her round pug eyes fixed on me as I fix a snack, as if to say, "Maybe if I look cute enough, she'll give me a treat."

Bebe can be so excited to see Charlie that she twists herself—and both their leashes—into a love knot in the middle of the street like two best friends reuniting, while trotting past two Golden Retrievers on a midwinter Sunday afternoon merits only a couple of nose bumps, canine equivalent of humans' "Hey, what's up?" As dogs keep their owners guessing, from minute to minute, how a passing scent, bird, or voice will affect them, so also we humans keep each other—and often, ourselves—in the dark about our true essences and preferences.

One of my favorite tea mugs--light blue with white polka-dots--features a black dog, nose pointed upward, and the words: "Be the person your dog thinks you are." It occurs to me that Bebe—most of the time—is fulfilling her end of the bargain, satisfying her Doggie Duty on earth. She stands guard against intruders, lives in the moment, and keeps her humans on their toes. From time to time, she likes a little treat, some play, a change of pace. Much as we help our animal friends and--while nuzzling their soft fur--crave the simplicity that they enjoy, they sense our potential, lest we forget. Perhaps the reverse side of my mug should read: "Be the person your angels know you will be," to remind me that, while I am unfurling yet another eco-friendly doggie waste bag, my heart should be lifting with the sight of the sun casting gold streaks across the sky as another day comes to an end.

But what really happened was that as I was finishing the last paragraph of this book, I heard a crash and some rustling from the direction of the kitchen. Springing from my chair to investigate, I found Domino's™[90] Dog chewing with gusto over an overturned pizza box that had been perched high on the counter, now containing only a forlorn-looking quarter of the pizza Gray had saved for me from Friday night's dinner. Bebe looked at me, licked her lips, and trotted away, leaving me to reheat the sad remnants in the microwave and marvel at how, once again, that dog got the last word.

ENDNOTES

[1] Julie Ann Turner is the bestselling author of the book *Genesis of Genius* and one of the world's leading authorities on the creative process.
[2] SCOOBY-DOO and all related characters and elements © & ™ Hanna-Barbera. (s18)
[3] From https://en.wikipedia.org/wiki/ZaSu_Pitts
[4] From https://en.wikipedia.org/wiki/Greed_(film)
[5] Product link (may not be available, ipad potty, Bed Bath & Beyond)
[6] Product link: *I Can Go Potty*, **Studio:** Consumervision **VHS Release Date:** October 9, 2001
[7] Dilbert comic strip by Scott Adams
[8] Seen on TV site
[9] Pat, Wikipedia link
[10] June Cleaver from *Leave It to Beaver*
[11] From Simply Irresistible, Songwriters: Robert Allan Palmer, 1988 Simply Irresistible lyrics © Warner/Chappell Music, Inc., Video
[12] Barbie's little sister.
[13] Emeril Lagasse, Wikipedia
[14] Wendy's "Where's the beef?" commercial, 1984, starring Clara Peller
[15] Galatians 6: 2; 7-9
[16] Enjoli: By Charles of the Ritz/Revlon.
[17] Enjoli name meaning
[18] Portmanteau definition - a linguistic blend of words,[1] in which parts of multiple words or their phones (sounds) are combined into a new word,[1][2][3] as in *smog*, coined by blending *smoke* and *fog*
[19] Aspercreme commercial
[20] Ebenezer Scrooge from Dickens' *A Christmas Carol*
[21] Charles Shultz' Peanuts comic strip's unseen character, the Great Pumpkin
[22] Walt Disney Company FastPass service
[23] Day of the Dead traditions
[24] La Calavera Catrina
[25] Astrologer Sydney Omarr books
[26] Songwriters: Galt Mac Dermot / James Rado / Gerome Ragni/1969/Album: The Age of Aquarius
Aquarius/Let the Sun Shine lyrics © Sony/ATV Music Publishing LLC
[27] Hair the musical; April, 2018 is the 50th anniversary of the debut of *Hair* on Broadway.
[28] The post was from a Facebook page called Looney Lane.

[29] "U Got the Look" by Prince, featuring Sheena Easton, from Sign 'o the Times, 1987 (Not to be confused with Roxette's "The Look" of 1989.)
[30] Songwriters: Danny Kortchmar/From the album *Building the Perfect Beast*, 1985
"All She Wants to Do Is Dance" lyrics © Warner/Chappell Music, Inc
[31] Great Scott! expression
[32] Pepperidge Farm bakery
[33] Archway molasses cookies
[34] Scott paper company
[35] "The Real Steele," by Leslie Bilodeau, published in the December 19, 1980 edition of the *ECHO*, student newspaper of East Catholic High School, Manchester, CT.
[36] "The Real Steele," by Leslie Bilodeau, published in the 1981 *ECLAT*, literary magazine of East Catholic High School, Manchester, CT.
[37] The gold building, One Financial Plaza, was built in 1975 and once housed the corporate headquarters of United Technologies Corporation. It's hard not to look at your reflection as you walk or drive by (much to the amusement, I'm sure, of those on the inside).
[38] WTIC stood for "Travelers Insurance Company," which owned the station until CBS took over. Hartford was known for being the "insurance capital," which sounded pretty boring to me but which would later dictate some of my (misguided but predictable) career choices.
[39] Datsun 510 Bluebird
[40] Strange Case of Dr. Jekyll and Mr. Hyde, by Robert Louis Stevenson
[41] Songwriters: Barrett Strong / Norman Whitfield
Papa Was a Rollin' Stone lyrics © Sony/ATV Music Publishing LLC
[42] *Lilias, Yoga, and You* show, aired in 1973 nationally on PBS (Public Broadcasting Service)
[43] Chaturanga illustration
[44] Saturn return definition
[45] Confucius quote
[46] The Pied Piper of Hamelin
[47] A *Rocky* moment
[48] A TRX suspension frame
[49] Mrs. Puff, from the Nickelodeon TV show *SpongeBob SquarePants*
[50] Based on six degrees of separation theory, using Safety Man instead of Kevin Bacon
[51] Silk City is a nickname for Manchester, CT
[52] Whac-a-mole game
[53] Forrest Gump stops running scene

⁵⁴ Dance Moms on Lifetime
⁵⁵ Curse of the Bambino
⁵⁶ Candid Camera
⁵⁷ The Beat Goes On Songwriters: Sonny Bono/1967
The Beat Goes On lyrics © Warner/Chappell Music, Inc
⁵⁸ Dalek, mutant extraterrestrials from the *Dr. Who* TV show
⁵⁹ ABC show from 1970s, Penny Marshall died in late 2018, played Laverne.
⁶⁰ Frieda, the curly-haired girl
⁶¹ Referring to *Alice's Adventures in Wonderland* by Lewis Carroll. Embarking upon a strange journey with many twists and turns, ending up (especially on the Web) somewhere far from where you started. https://www.dictionary.com/e/slang/rabbit-hole/
⁶² Lestoil information
⁶³ https://www.poetryfoundation.org/poems/43189/song-of-the-witches-double-double-toil-and-trouble
⁶⁴ 1978 Lestoil commercial
⁶⁵ Lyrics from The Candy Man, by Sammy Davis, Jr. (Song written for the 1971 movie *Willy Wonka & The Chocolate Factory*, based on the book *Charlie and the Chocolate Factory* by Roald Dahl)
⁶⁶ Let sleeping dogs lie
⁶⁷ Grover book
⁶⁸ Mr. Rogers' Neighborhood
⁶⁹ Quote from Working Girl
⁷⁰ The Cat in the Hat, by Dr. Seuss
⁷¹ Undercover Boss TV show
⁷² Benjamin Franklin quote
⁷³ Yogi Berra quote
⁷⁴ The Wizard of Oz movie
⁷⁵ Gina McCarthy, who served as Commissioner of the CT Department of Environment Protection from 2004-2009 and was the 13th Administrator of the EPA from July, 2013-January, 2017.
⁷⁶ Don Quixote, novel by Miguel de Cervantes
⁷⁷ *Man of La Mancha* is a musical first performed at the Goodspeed Opera House in East Haddam, CT in 1965, then on Broadway.
⁷⁸ Mrs. Doubtfire, 1993 film
⁷⁹ Edgar Allan Poe, "The Tell-Tale Heart"
⁸⁰ Referring to the style of Sir Alfred Hitchcock's films
⁸¹ From the First Letter of Paul to the Corinthians, 12:31
⁸² From Luke 12:43
⁸³ 1970s Crying Indian PSA
⁸⁴ Discover card commercial

[85] A Family Affair, late 1960s TV show
[86] Leslie speaker inventor
[87] Datsun 510
[88] Dueling Banjos
[89] Songwriters: Bill Danoff / John Denver / Taffy Nivert Danoff "Take Me Home, Country Roads" lyrics © Kobalt Music Publishing Ltd., BMG Rights Management, Reservoir Media Management Inc
[90] Domino's pizza with peppers and olives, my favorite

www.ingramcontent.com/pod-product-compliance
Lightning Source LLC
Chambersburg PA
CBHW031103080526
44587CB00011B/797